Intercultural Interacting

V. Lynn Tyler

David M. Kennedy Center for International Studies
Brigham Young University

Originally published as *Intercultural Communicating*,
© 1979 BYU, David M. Kennedy Center for International Studies

BYU, David M. Kennedy Center for International Studies,
Publication Services, 280 HRCB, Provo, Utah 84602

Library of Congress Cataloging-in-Publication Data

Tyler, V. Lynn.
    Intercultural interacting.

    1. Intercultural communication. 2. Interpersonal relations.
I. Title.
HM258.T94   1987   303.4'82   86–32704
ISBN 0–912575–05–0

Table of Contents

Acknowledgements

Writers of books
    can easily agree
    with one of my
        many mentors,
Mary Ritchie Key,
that we all stand
    on the shoulders
    of our predecessors
    and benefactors
    and associates;
yet, in our acknowledgement
    of the past,
    we do not want the future
    to be blinded by
    previous misconceptions
        or inadequacies.

With Mary, I would
    be appreciative
        of past findings and
at the same time
be sprightly imaginative
    and adventurous
in creating and setting up
    explorations
for what our future
    with other people holds.
Indeed, we will rarely find
    the quarks of
    acceptable human interaction
    without building alone
        and together
    on secured research.

Another of my insightful
    teacher-friends,
Sy Fersh, has
    tutored some of us

on the need
    not only for
    pre-paration but
    post-paration—
        to pair our desirable
        cultural experiences
with tomorrow
    as well as
    today
and to know
    such experiences
    are favorable.
(If you get the chance,
ask Sy about *shibui*
and *omoiyari* too.)

When the first try at
    the topic this little
    volume treats began,
it was known as
    Into Intercultural
    Communication and
appeared at
    Michael Prosser's
        Massanetta Springs,
        Virginia, conference.

Fellow people-to-peoplers
    at that long ago event
        were kind in offering
        suggestions for what
came to be the
    experiential learning aid
    Intercultural
    Communicating.

A decade later, after
    many willing users

have shared their
"post-parations"
with that interaction
tool, we now look
at what may be
even more useful
sets of ideators and
feeling-facilitators.

Close colleagues
L Robert Kohls,
Beulah F. Rohrlich,
and Robert T. Moran
have catalyzed much in the
ideas now found here
but originating in
our many sharing-times.

SIETAR-International friends
and fellow explorers
have, in myriad
unrecorded ways,
tempered approaches
herewith suggested.

My good fortune in having
research associates
and refiners
reminds me of my
indebtedness to Janet Thomas,
Paula K.Boothe, David Hatch,
Marshall S. Witt, Gail A.
Newbold, Peggy H. Smith,
Pamela D. Jackson,
Lynn B. Jenson,
Veronique Longmire, and to
Paul Taylor, David Pace,
Martina S. Aleson, Malia Howland,
Randy McClarren.

Ernest Wilkins, James S. Taylor,
R. Max Rogers, Spencer J. Palmer,
Stan A. Taylor, and Ray C. Hillam

have allowed the creative time
and resources necessary
for even mini-tools
such as this to appear.

May the users feel significant
gratitude, with me.

My bride Arlean and our children
patiently and
contributively have
endured the testing
required by
developing exercises.

And my gracious colleague
Debbie Coon
has creatively helped
give birth to the
many components—
such as *Culturgrams*
and *Infograms*—
from which
Intercultural Interacting
finds your attention.

To each, and to all others
who have edited,
suffered through,
and critiqued these
humble "keys to success,"
I offer my gratitude
and implore that help
which makes efforts
like this
re-do-able.

You are included!

Mahalo and ALOHA!
V. Lynn Tyler
Provo, Utah
Autumn 1986

Preface

Interacting with individuals from another culture is often a serious matter. It can be arduous. It is always complex. In this concise, up-dated book, Lynn Tyler explains the process in a clear, thoughtfully arranged, engaging, even amusing manner. After absorbing the lessons of the book, the conscientious reader will be more careful in approaching intercultural interaction, but also more perceptive and more confident.

"People in culture-contact situations frequently fail to really understand each other." This judgment, made by Edward Hall, is one of the many pertinent quotations incorporated into the book. Quite a lot has now been written on the fact that we fail. Much less is available on what to do about our failures. On the pages which follow, Lynn outlines, often step by step, what we can do.

"Where do you begin to understand the peoples of the world?" Lynn asks. No question could be more fundamental. The insights and procedures he recommends here provide an excellent place to start. "How can we encourage empathy, communication, shared ideas, and experiences?" he also asks. Surely many of us must become better at this if ethnic, racial, and national violence are to be avoided and diverse, potentially conflicting human resources are to be integrated. But how? A practical strategy is needed. In each chapter which follows, important parts of the strategy are suggested.

Because this book analyzes interaction at a very basic level, and because it describes concrete situations involving individuals in different roles, the book will be appreciated and used by readers with a variety of needs, concerns, and priorities. It is relevant to teachers and students as well as tourists and expatriates, government officials, missionaries, counselors, and others whose professions require creative contact with cultures unlike their own.

Appropriately, this volume is not only *about* interaction. It *creates* interaction—between the author and the reader. The author addresses us directly and challenges us to reflect and make decisions. Frequently, he asks us questions. Then, as he advises us to do ourselves, he respectfully questions our answers.

We therefore learn about interaction not only through facts, figures and abstract analysis, but primarily through the process of interaction itself. The goal is "to develop workable perspectives and skills." One key, Lynn explains, is that "you humbly pay the price of researching important information about other people." For many years Lynn, himself, has paid this price. And he has certainly done it humbly. During the years he has learned about, from, and with many individuals from dramatically differing cultures, just as he urges us to do. Now he shares with us the tested guidelines which have served him so well. Through this book many of us can benefit from his constant exertion and from all he has invested over the years.

Another key, Lynn demonstrates, is that "you use creative feedback from other people and give it as well, as a positive growth factor. No one in the intercultural field has requested as much feedback as frequently as Lynn. What he offers us here, therefore, is not only the result of his own expenditure, experience, and insight, but also that of the many seasoned men and women in the field who have responded to his openness.

This carefully-worded, recently up-dated study reflects, in additon, important developments in the intercultural field during the last ten years. Like parts of the field now, it is more systematic, more practical, and more professional. Like the best writing in the field now, this guide is based on a better understanding of the needs and limitations of practitioners in the field, while, at the same time, demanding more of us.

Intercultural interactions, as Lynn portrays them, can be enriching, expanding, and great fun. Usually they are also very exacting. One point that becomes clear as readers work through their learning exercises is that interacting effectively with individuals from contrasting cultures requires a thorough preparation, a constant determination, and a keen attention to detail which many Americans have heretofore devoted only to their technical tasks. In other words, the development of true intercultural competence requires a new kind of self-discipline.

Clear, too, from Lynn's contributions here, is the fact that intercultural transactions carry new and complicated responsibilities. We are called on to understand deeply, to interpret accurately, to represent fairly, to care constructively, and to be accountable for the consequences—both negative and positive—of our initiatives and reactions. This all boils down to a simple truth: *we are often responsible for others' response to us*. Americans, given our desire for autonomy and self-sufficiency, seldom recognize this and are inclined to avoid such responsibility. This is a major reason why we are surprised by other people's attitudes and actions toward us. Our blindness in this area is a serious handicap in our relations with both individuals and nations. Anyone who investigates, participates, and evaluates as Lynn recommends here will have to come to terms with this responsibility.

For more years than most of us, Lynn has been trying, with extraordinary commitment, to "open doors to understanding and friendship." In the practical recommendations and exercises which follow, he opens a number of critical doors. Furthermore, showing his readers the respect and trust he rightly says are essential to effective communciation, he encourages us, and enables us, to go beyond this book and open still more doors as we continue on our fascinating, fruitful journeys.

George W. Renwick, President
Renwick and Associates

Chapter 1

Keys to Successful Interacting

What is this all about? Perhaps you have had rewarding—or frustrating—experiences in other cultures before. Almost everyone does.

You may be preparing now for your first crossing into unfamiliar national or people boundaries. Whether or not you are new at intercultural communication and interaction, the exercises and resources that follow can help you bridge differences and surmount barriers that too often exist between different peoples.

What will it take to open the doors to understanding and friendship in new cultural settings? How can you better understand and deal with unique intercultural encounters?

Because people of one culture generally think, feel, act, and express themselves differently than those of another, successful interaction requires us to learn carefully about, and to deal well with both our own and others' values, perspectives, predispositons, expectations, and activities.

A formidable task, you say? Relax. It begins very naturally. As you become a "people-to-people ambassador," you will be able to understand your own working world view as well as those of peoples in other places.

As you move beyond your usual and normal cultural bias (ethnocentrism), your actions can enhance rather than hinder your experiences with different people and circumstances. You can become a global citizen.

How can you develop workable perspectives and skills in your encounters, especially when others might also be biased or have needs that you might not be able to meet? By working through this learning aid, you can teach yourself how, when, and with whom to use specific interaction skills. While some of these skills will be acquired *before* you enter other cultures, others can best be developed *during* your encounters. Still others will help you *after* each experience.

1

Keys

You develop real empathy for the feelings, values, needs, and insights of other people. (They become comfortable as they recognize your understanding and feeling for what concerns them.)

Your interaction is flexible, positive, and pleasant, as is apparent by your good will and sincerity. (You and they Co-mmunicate!)

You humbly pay the price of researching important information about other people, including their perceptions and expressions, and how you can learn *from* and *with* them. (Interdependence and balance are recognized.)

You suspend unnecessary judgments until essential facts are determined and possible outcomes are assessed. (In emergencies, you demonstrate calmness and a willingness to cooperate appropriately.)

You use caution if criticism is necessary and give praise that is both acceptable and sincere. (You learn and practice what is best in public and in private, as well as how to respond to criticism and praise directed at you. You tolerate mistakes, and allow growth.)

You invite trust, by keeping the confidences of those with whom you interact. (As much as possible, you avoid embarrassing yourself or others.)

You use creative feedback from other people and give it as well, as a positive growth factor. (You reveal a lot about yourself when you show others that you care. Feelings often count more than logic or data—particularly if you *listen* reflectively and honestly.)

The ideas and exercises in this booklet will help you explore a wide variety of interactions that can either prevent or enhance effective interaction. More than anything, as you practice the principles that you learn, you will continually teach yourself how to deal with significant similiarities and differences, with bridges and gaps, with familiarity and openness, all of which are illustrated in the people patterns we call culture.

Browse quickly through this booklet, noting ideas you want to develop, and set some realistic goals for yourself. Then come back to these keys after your learning experiences. Decide which keys you feel comfortable with as you make the "foreign" become familiar.

The greatest enemy of intercultural understanding is its own illusion.

(Adapted from Peace Corps adage)

Chapter 2

Becoming People-to-People Ambassadors

Face it: whether you are going on that dream trip come true, on an extended or brief international assignment, or simply to interact with foreign neighbors or visitors, you will have mixed feelings. Despite any reservations you have, you will have many opportunities for enriching experiences, expanded horizons, and continued self-development.

You Are a People-to-People Ambassador

Being a host or guest in another culture is a responsibility. In a real sense, you are presenting your culture and country as well as yourself. You may be one of only a few people from your culture that others come to know. Their attitudes and opinions will be influenced by how you react to them and their way of thinking, feeling, and acting. How concerned are you about avoiding embarrassing situations, projecting a positive image, and coping with change without negatively affecting others?

Apprehension about the unfamiliar is very real. "What will it be like? Will I be able to adjust quickly?" Sound familiar? By being aware of and dealing with the impressions you are forming about others, and impressions they are forming about you, you naturally become a people-to-people ambassador. We can guarantee a meaningful and invaluable experience.

The term "American" may be misleading; it can refer to anyone from North, Central, or South America. For our purposes, the term "American" will refer to a citizen of the United States.

Which is "Better"?

Cultures, even within our own country, are unique. We are all unique people. But there are recognizable patterns among peoples' language, customs, food, dress, religion, philosophy, and reactions to basic situations. It is normal for people to feel that their own way of doing things is better than any other. This is *ethnocentrism*—the concept that one's own culture is of central importance and is a proper basis for judging other peoples and cultures. Perhaps when you see things done differently in other cultures, you will catch yourself thinking, "Back home we know how to do it right." Ask yourself, "Why is it right?" You will probably be forced to rationalize, "I don't know; it's just better." Ethnocentrism is normal; it is sometimes patriotic and acceptable—as long as it is not imposed on other people, when it becomes a negative influence. Every person is entitled to his or her own world view, self-esteem, cultural pride, and dignity. Understanding this idea is imperative for an ambassador, so that misunderstanding and offense can be avoided.

> *The American or the foreigner may not be aware of his own assumptions or the dominant patterns of his own culture. Such misunderstanding is more likely to produce violated expectations, continued mistrust, inflexibility, and superficial problem solving. On the other hand, mutual understanding yields confirmation of expectations, trust realistic with conditions, and more creative, effective and productive problem solving.*
>
> (Bernard Bass)

Take A Good Look At Yourself

No doubt you have already learned something about what you will be doing and what the people and conditions will be like. Such preparation is very important. As you begin to understand *them*, you also need to better understand *yourself*. When you recognize that you are a product of your own culture, you find others' behaviors, attitudes, values, and beliefs more acceptable—or at least tolerable, and your adjustment will be easier.

Take a good look at yourself by "mapping" what you think is most important to you, why you feel good about what you do and want to accomplish. What in your personality seems to help or hinder your interactions with others at home? How do you handle confrontations, giving and receiving gifts, visiting and receiving visitors, delay, or distress? How well do you cope during crises?

We will see how to creatively "map" other people later, but for now, take time to determine *who you are* and *why,* as a prelude to your intercultural encounters ahead.

Mapping can help you realize just how unique and fortunate you are—a culturally oriented person with the capability of becoming a people-to-people ambassador of understanding and friendship.

Although this booklet is directed to those who are visiting or living in other cultures, the exercises can also be useful for encounters with visitors of one's own culture. The more people and cultures involved, the more challenging—and rewarding—the experience.

> *Intercultural communication: when it is effective the results can be very dramatic; when it is not, the results can also be very dramatic.*
>
> (Source unknown)

6

Chapter 3

Will the Real "Right Way"
Please Stand Up?

> *If other people do not make the conclusions we do, they must somehow be confused, uneducated, peculiar, or simply wrong.*
>
> (John C. Condon)

Is there anything worse than doing the wrong thing at the wrong time? When interacting with people of different cultures, doing the wrong thing at the wrong time may be not only embarrassing but also offensive. Significant differences do exist between cultures; it can be fun to learn about and work with them. The following exercise is designed to help you realize that the people and culture of your own country can seem as "different" to others as theirs do to you.

> *Those who will not see are at a greater loss than those who cannot see.*
>
> (Source unknown)

Choose the answer you consider most appropriate in the following situations.

7

Conversing

1. In casual conversation you should stand an arm's distance from the other person.

2. In casual conversation you should stand very close—within a foot—and as you talk, you should search the other person's face.

A dead giveaway? You probably selected the first answer unless you have had experience with people from the Middle East or Latin America. In many cultures, two to four feet away is the polite and customary distance in casual conversations. Some people, Americans for example, would consider a closer distance between casual friends to be rude or strange. But in many Middle Eastern cultures it is a sign of politeness to let an acquaintance feel your breath as you talk. But situations vary; you will find it helpful, when appropriate, to follow the guideline, "When in Rome, do as the Romans do."

Working

1. After working all day at your job, you should stay and socialize with your co-workers, and plan to leave for home at seven or eight in the evening.

2. After working all day at your job, the time is yours to spend with your family, or however you wish.

If you are American, the second answer was most likely your choice. As a general rule, Americans are very possessive of their free time. They like to choose what they do "after hours." After finishing a day on the job, you may choose to go home or to linger and socialize, but the choice must exist.

But what if you are Japanese? In Japan, many workers are expected to socialize after work, in a group sport for example. Work relations extend to such social interactions.

Public Display of Affection

1. It is unacceptable for two men to hold hands as they walk together in public.

2. It is appropriate for two men to hold hands in public as they walk together.

What is your first reaction when you see two men walking down the street holding hands? Because of your culture, you may feel uncomfortable about it unless one of them needs physical assistance. But in some cultures, it is acceptable and common for men, women, and children of all ages to hold hands in public. It's done, and it's not unusual. The meaning Americans place on such an action results from American culture, and does not necessarily apply to other peoples.

Responding to Questions

1. It is better to avoid a direct and forthright answer to some questions by skirting the subject and then leading up to it gradually and indirectly.

2. Being direct and forthright is an admirable quality because it shows that you are honest and unafraid to say what you believe. Many questions demand a direct answer.

Would you be surprised to learn that in many countries it is often considered more polite to skirt a subject and arrive at it indirectly? Simply (and forthrightly) stated, directness can be seen as a lack of finesse.

Showing Agreement

1. If you are in agreement with another person, you nod your head up and down.

2. If you are in agreement with another person, you raise your eyebrows.

No, we're not kidding. Ask certain Pacific Islanders a question to be answered in the affirmative. To many people, including some Polynesians, nodding your head does not indicate a positive response, as you might think. What means "yes" to some can mean "no" to others.

Accepting Praise

1. A person being publicly congratulated for excellent personal performance would feel complimented and have an incentive to continue excelling.

2. A person who is publicly congratulated for excellent personal performance would feel offended because group identification is more important than individual accomplishment, and to be singled out is to be ostracized from the group.

Do you pride yourself on your individuality? An acquaintance from the Far East most likely lives in a culture in which the group is more important than any individual—including himself.

Consider other reasons why individuals might react negatively to an award or commendation. Remember, their perceptions may be based on the answers they give to the following questions. How might they respond?

> What have they accomplished, not only now, but over the years?
> What motive might be perceived about you for giving an award?
> Do you expect additional action from the recipient in return for the acknowledgement?
> Did you give the compliment, commmendation, or award solely to acknowledge or praise a job well done; or did you mean it to serve as pressure, leverage, manipulation, or even a bribe?

In any culture, it is important to consider how and why recipients view different forms of recognition.

When is a Wave Goodbye a Wave Goodbye?

Even though it's a small world, there is likely not a single gesture, facial expression, or custom that means *exactly* the same thing worldwide. People in some cultures use gestures and expressions the same way you do. But meanings that seem obvious to us are often misunderstood or misinterpreted by others. Here are a few examples of such differences between cultures:

1. The *handshake* is a common greeting in America for meeting both men and women. To many Asians—even those familair with the American practice—it is not polite to shake hands with women or children. On the other hand (no pun intended), in Germanic Europe courtesy dictates that you shake hands with almost everyone, both when arriving and departing.

2. Is it a natural gesture for you to acknowledge a child by patting him or her on the head, or an acquaintance with a pat on the back? Be careful. In Thailand and other Far Eastern countries where the head is considered sacred, it is very offensive to touch another person's head. Even touching a friend's back in public may indicate overfamiliarity.

3. The simple gesture of waving goodbye doesn't always mean farewell. If you wave goodbye to some South Americans or South Asians by holding the palm down and wagging the fingers, they may return and ask what else you want rather than leave. In many countries, the gesture meaning "come here" is made with the palm down, much like the American way of waving goodbye.

4. To be seen as honest and forthright, Americans typically look directly at people they speak to. If you feel someone has lied to you, you might even say, "He couldn't look me straight in the eye." But in many cultures, lowered eyes are not an admission of guilt or a sign of discomfort, but indicate an attitude of respect.

Even in the U.S. it is often considered impolite to look directly at a person for very long (unless of course that person is performing or delivering a speech). This may be why Americans sometimes interpret the Frenchman's tendency to hold a gaze as being forward.

5. When introducing your family, do you include the children? In some countries, the children are not introduced out of respect to adults. Thus in a different culture, greeting children can prove to be unexpected and awkward. People might not know how to respond.

6. Nodding the head up and down to indicate "yes" and shaking the head from side to side to mean "no" may seem to be universally accepted signs. But in some parts of Bulgaria, India, and the Middle East, nodding the head means "no," while shaking it from side to side means "yes" or "maybe".

7. In Europe, if you were trying to ask a ticket clerk for one ticket, would you raise your index finger to indicate that you want one? If so, you would be surprised to be given two. In Europe, number one is usually indicated by the extended thumb. In other countries, the American finger count for two (first and second fingers in a V-shape) may be offensive. This gesture should generally be avoided unless you are certain of local meanings. (This is also true of the symbol for "O.K.," with fingers and thumb in a circle—an obscene gesture in several countries, a sign of zero or disapproval in others.)

Miscues and Missed Cues

Learn what gestures, stances, and expressions communicate in the culture you will visit—which gestures are common to both cultures, and which are only "yours" or "theirs." Be aware that certain gestures do not always communicate, or that they can miscommunicate, and you can avoid awkward moments.

"So just what *can* I rely on when I go to another country?" you ask. "If symbols mean different things, if facial expressions do not mean what I think they mean, how will I know if I am making myself understood, or if I'm offending others? In short, how can I know what people are really feeling and thinking?" Good questions. Let's see about answering them.

Though nonverbal expressions differ from culture to culture, certain feelings and emotions do not. Almost everyone responds favorably to concern and trust. Likewise, almost everyone is upset by indifference or antagonism. In general, people love their parents and friends, are respectful of certain members of their society, and

12

are concerned with providing food, clothing, and shelter for their families. *The difference is that diverse cultures have different ways of interpreting and showing these universal feelings.* You need to learn the unfamiliar ways. Consider, for example, what angers you may not disturb an Asian (and vice versa). Ways of showing emotion often differ between cultures.

Don't panic. Though you may not entirely understand the ways of a culture, the people can tell you what they are feeling and thinking through their reactions, behaviors, orientations, communication patterns, and lifestyles. They will always give feedback. It is your responsibility to understand what is going on in a given situation.

The way people communicate in other cultures is just as effective and "correct" as the way you communicate. Think about it. When you are the visitor, *you* are the one who is different! Learning basic expressions in the local language can help you overcome some of the communication problems. Learning what is polite and acceptable is essential. Some customs, gestures, and behaviors may be common in their culture as well as yours; others are unique.

Aside from "being looked at," you have the responsibility of "looking at"—that is, of evaluating as well as being evaluated. You may have some preconceived ideas about what Germans, Nigerians, or Koreans are like, just as many people throughout the world have stereotyped notions about Americans. If you suspend judgment and take time to look at yourself and others, you will learn more about yourself and your own culture and other cultures.

Be flexible. Temporarily suspending judgment of every aspect of a different culture is impossible. There is no way you can entirely keep from judging the people, their language, dress patterns, family life, or work habits. But, we suggest that you avoid drawing premature conclusions about the foreign culture as a whole. Negative generalizations eventually result in a narrower understanding.

How do you suspend judgment? There is no easy answer to this one. But start by trying to separate yourself from negative aspects of your own ethnocentrism. Be less subjective in examining the foreign culture, while at the same time reexamining your own culture. This does not mean you must give up being who you are. On the contrary, you will make others feel uncomfortable if you try to be something you are not. Even so, you may be confused if it appears that the local people expect you to act like them, especially if sometimes they expect you to act very differently than they do. They may even treat you in ways that are not acceptable in their own culture. What is socially acceptable often will depend on the situation and the people involved.

> *It is so much a part of so many of us that sometimes we forget its powerful effect on our ways of thinking, feeling, communicating. Tradition— find out about it!*
>
> (Source unknown)

Though you can't live exactly as you do in your own culture, it is inappropriate to try to live exactly like the people in the culture you are visiting. You will need to find a balance between maintaining your own identity and avoiding "cultural imperialism." How does one achieve such a balance? You need to perceive yourself as a people-to-people ambassador, bridging the gap between cultures, not with "my ways" or "their ways," but "*our* ways."

> *True communication forces us to question our old ways of dealing with it.*
>
> (Anonymous)

Chapter 4

Americans: Beyond Apple Pie, Baseball, Pizza, and Tacos

You have certain appetites, attitudes, feelings, and reactions that are distinctly American. This is because you have more in common with members of your own society than with people of other nations. For instance, you use certain idiomatic expressions; you shop in the same kinds of stores; you participate in similar kinds of recreation; you have gone to the same kinds of schools; you experience similar kinds of television, radio, and newspaper coverage; and you are accustomed to certain kinds of reactions from people in given situations. These similarities bind people together into a cultural or national society.

But, when we discuss the similarities among citizens of a country, we don't mean that the people are just millions of carbon copies of one type.

The following discussion of some American characteristics gives examples of how lifestyles between cultures can vary. Examples of how your own culture varies from others should come to mind.

Put yourself in the role of a typical American. Each case study describes an American attitude and contrasts it with a different culture.

Think through the possible reactions and the potential results of each.

Case I
Standards of Living

You are a young American man who has just graduated with a Master's degree in business administration.

You were raised in a split-level brick home in a subdivision of a midwestern city. While you were growing up, you shared a bedroom with your brother; your two younger sisters had rooms of their own.

When you were old enough to drive, you used the second car—the one Mom used for shopping and taking your sister to piano lessons—to drive to school and on dates.

Your family had a color television, dishwasher, a clothes washer and dryer, two telephones, and other "luxuries" in your home. While you were in college, Mom refurnished the living room and Dad remodeled the garage to make a work area where he could tinker with his woodworking tools.

You were married last year. You and your wife have been living in a duplex. Your apartment has two bedrooms, one of which is being used as a study and workroom. You don't have a dishwasher, but you share a clothes washer and dryer with the other family in the duplex. You have a portable television and a stereo, and you are buying your own car.

You have been offered a management position in an overseas branch of a large company, and you fly over for some preliminary meetings. Karl, a native of the country who will be an associate in your office, invites you to dinner with his family at his home.

During your visit you have found the city picturesque and the old architecture beautiful, but had not thought of people living in those old buildings until the taxi pulls up in front of a gray, four-story building that looks several centuries old. You climb the cement staircase to the third floor and walk down a dimly lit hall to Karl's apartment.

As you visit, you learn that Karl has no car; he takes the bus to work. He has been waiting a year to have a telephone installed, and a small television set just fits in the corner of the living room. The kitchen is tiny, so Karl's wife serves sandwiches in the living room. She explains that all meals are served on the small table at which you are seated. Further conversation reveals that the children sleep on rollaway beds in an all-purpose storage room and that the couch folds out into a bed for the husband and wife.

What do you think as you ride home that evening?

[ ] "I'd never ask my wife to live like this! She'd die without some room to move around in. Surely there must be some homes or apartments comparable to our duplex at home."

[ ] "How can people live like this? It's disgusting! Doesn't Karl want something better for his famly?"

[ ] "Karl's salary is about the same as mine, yet he's limited to this small apartment. Does this mean I might have trouble finding the kind of living arrangements I'd like?"

[ ] "How depressing! I can't enjoy socializing in these cramped quarters. When we're living here, I'll be sure to avoid any further dinner invitations from Karl."

Any of these reactions might characterize an American experiencing a foreign culture for the first time. Although Americans constitute only six percent of the world's population, they consume a large percentage of the world's resources. Many products that Americans consider necessities are luxuries in other countries. Most Americans think that such things as televisions, cars, telephones, washers and dryers, and lots of space are indispensable.

Although you may not consider yourself wealthy, you have things that only the most well-to-do people have in most cultures. Not everyone in America is financially independent, but the middle-class value system insists that everyone should try to be "a success." Success is often assessed in terms of possessions. No doubt Karl is as interested in providing his family with the comforts and conveniences of life as you are, but the economic conditions of his country limit his ability to provide the things that are within easy reach of most middle-class Americans.

You will find it necessary to modify your lifestyle in this new culture. Although your salary is sufficient to allow for the purchase of an automobile, you may find it more convenient to use public transportation. More spacious living quarters probably exist, but they are probably much more expensive than Karl's small apartment. The fact that you can afford a telephone may not make it easy to obtain one—perhaps you will be placed on a waiting list. Obviously you won't find everything just the way it was "back home." You may have to reconcile yourself to some inconvenience and changes in routine.

Case II
Manual Labor

You are a middle-aged American housewife living in a split-level home similar to that described in Case I. Your husband's father was a farmer in your midwestern state. Many years ago your husband, Harold, left the farm to work as a stockboy for a department store. Now he is general manager of that store.

You both worked and sacrificed in the early years of your marriage to provide your children with material comforts, especially with the opportunity for an education and the improved life a good education offers. Your two sons have graduated from college, and one daughter is working part-time to finance her university education. Another daughter married shortly after graduation from high school; however, she received training as a beautician and she runs a small beauty shop in the basement of her home.

Although you worked during part of your married life, you are now able to spend the day at home. You have had time to take an adult-education class in interior decorating, which helped you refurnish your living room, and you learned how to make gifts and wall decorations in lessons offered by a craft store. When your house was built, your husband did all the landscaping, and continues to do the yardwork. Recently, he bought a woodworking set that he spends a lot of time with.

Your family is hosting an international student, Magda, from the Middle East, who is attending the university with your daughter. She has been living with you for two weeks now. You have an opportunity to ask her about herself, her country, and the lifestyle there.

Magda reminds you that her family is rather well-to-do in comparison with the majority of her countrymen. She has never done any kind of manual work in the home. They have always had maids to do the cooking and cleaning. Her father, who, like your husband, is the manager of a prosperous business, wouldn't think of doing any repair or maintenance work around the home. He hires a carpenter, plumber, electrician, gardener, or general laborer, depending on the job he needs done.

She is surprised to learn that your husband worked himself up from a farmer's son to a successful executive. She explains that in her country, people must be satisfied with the position and status into which they are born. One born into a lower class has difficulty attaining wealth or social status. Educational opportunities are increasingly available to children on all levels of society, but this does not significantly affect the movement of an individual from lower to upper levels of the social scale.

As you contemplate your conversation with Magda, what are your thoughts?

[ ] "No wonder Magda never lifts a finger to help around the house! She's been spoiled rotten!"

[ ] "What a backward country she comes from. It must be a dictatorship—trying to keep the poor people ignorant so that the wealthy and influential people can exploit them."

[ ] "I guess in her country we'd just be considered peasants who got lucky. I'll bet she even thinks of herself as being far above us in social status—just because Harold was born on a farm. She makes it sound like it's a crime to improve your life through hard work."

[ ] "I respect her background, but she must learn to respect ours. How can I help her realize that our lifestyle requires some manual labor without offending her?"

Americans, with some exceptions, believe that success can be achieved through hard work—that people can overcome their environment and heredity. Wishing for a better life is valid to the American only if the wish is followed by action directed toward a goal. Americans seek tangible results and practical applications from their dreams.

Americans are typically competitive and aggressive. They take pride in breaking records set by others. This attitude reflects their emphasis on personal achievement, especially in their jobs. There is no stigma attached to a person's rising above the station into which they were born. Indeed, the poor or underprivileged person who "pulls himself up by his bootstraps" and achieves success in business, politics, or finance is viewed as a hero and becomes almost legendary in America.

Americans are seen as always busy—working hard and playing hard, even when they're on vacation. The United States is one of the few countries in which people of all social classes engage in physical labor, working in their yards and doing their own housework.

Because of these American values and beliefs, you may view Magda's lifestyle as undesirable or repressive. But doesn't Magda find certain things equally undesirable in the United States? You may think she isn't doing her share of the housework because she's been "spoiled." Could it be that her culture has taught her to view manual labor quite differently than you do? What other attitudes of hers seem to clash with yours? Does the fact that these perspectives differ make one "good" and the other "bad"? One "right" and the other "wrong"?

Educational opportunities and systems vary greatly between countries. In the United States education is available to all and is considered extremely important. The education system is oriented toward competition and winning; practical thinking is highly valued. The expansion of college education has, on the whole, reduced educational inequalities in terms of sex, race, religion, and income. The expanded facilities for higher education are used primarily by young people. Correspondence and night schools have emerged for adults. Americans are encouraged from childhood to be independent, to make decisions, and to develop their creativity.

Obviously the educational system in Magda's country is quite different. We might justifiably consider it unfortunate that education is not available to all, but it is unwise for us to make judgments about why this condition exists or how it could be remedied.

Case III
Age, Aging, and the Aged

You are a seventeen-year-old American boy. Your father is a high school science teacher and your mother works for a real estate agency. You have two younger brothers.

Your father is 42. He works hard to keep in shape and he recently joined a health spa, where he works out several times a week. He is balding and your mother is trying to talk him into getting a toupee. Your mother is 40 and also works hard to keep a youthful appearance. She has her hair done weekly and has been using a rinse to hide the gray.

Your father's parents live in a nearby town. They visit occasionally, usually on holidays and birthdays. Your mother's parents live thousands of miles away. They are old, and you see them once or twice a year—at a family reunion or when your family takes a vacation to their state. Because of your grandparents' age, and because no other relatives live near them, your parents are considering bringing them to your town, where they could live comfortably in a nearby rest home.

After high-school graduation, you spend a summer abroad. In the Chang household, the father's parents live with the family and are treated with the utmost respect. They are sought after for their wise counsel. Three teenage children and two cousins also live with this family.

You've observed your parents' efforts to look younger and have heard them complain about the fact that they are aging. The couple you live with, on the other hand, are looking forward to growing old. They are proud of their gray hair and feel it a sign of their arrival at an age where they will be able to live with their children and receive love and respect.

As you compare your family relationship to theirs, what are your impressions? Any of the following?

[ ] "I don't like living with all these people: grandparents, aunts, uncles, and cousins. Shouldn't they be in their own homes?"

[ ] "Dad sure looks great compared to Mr. Chang. Mrs. Chang loves to cook as much as her husband loves to eat. No wonder he's so fat."

[ ] "Mrs. Chang is really quite pretty. I wonder why she doesn't fix herself up a bit. That gray in her hair makes her look as old as a Grandma."

[ ] "It's kind of nice having some other family members nearby. I never appreciated before all that my grandparents could teach me—if I only knew them better."

You have different attitudes toward youth and age than the Changs do. In the United States, *youth* is the magic word. It is desirable to be young (late teens to early thirties). Advertising tries to associate products with attractive, youthful people, and many products are designed to help the American look and feel younger. Older people often try to keep the illusion of youth by wearing the clothes of younger generations. The general attitude is that growing old is undesirable. Usually older people are respected only if they can communicate and interact well with younger people, or if they are famous.

What appears to be the Chang's carelessness about maintaining their youthful appearance is a reflection of the attitude toward age in their culture. In their way of thinking, there is great value in being and appearing older. Mrs. Chang is not "letting herself go" by not covering her gray hair, nor is Mr. Chang ignoring modern fashion by not being concerned about his weight.

Were you also annoyed or surprised to find so many relatives living under the same roof? The American family is generally a two-generation group: mom and dad and the kids. If grandparents live nearby, they are probably only occasional guests in the home. Older relatives are often placed in rest homes. Apparently in the country you are visiting, caring for the aged is a family privilege as well as a responsibility. This responsibility extends to more distant relatives also.

Case IV
Freedom and Democracy

You are an American civil engineer. In recent years you have been concerned about the increasing amount of welfare being distributed by the state and national government. As one who strongly believes in earning his own way through life, you have resented "freeloaders" who want "something for nothing."

You are assigned to supervise a building project in another country. Shortly after arriving there, you are informed that you must register with the police in the city. If you move to another city, you must check out of the first city and register with the new police department. You also learn that you are living in a socialistic society that has a strong central political party. Medical care is completely socialized. Education is also free. Welfare assistance is readily available to all who are unemployed or in need.

In looking for an apartment, you find that you cannot live in some apartments you like because they are part of a federally funded housing project and available only to citizens of that country. You also learn that monopolies control most large businesses.

What do you think of all this?

[ ] "What a bunch of freeloaders! Don't they realize what their government is doing to them?"

[ ] "All this free stuff might be great for them, but what about me? It's pure discrimination! If I get sick, I pay an outrageous bill. If I want decent housing, I have to pay outrageous rent because government housing is closed to me."

[ ] "Register with the police? I've never been so insulted! What do they think I am, a spy? I'm going to the American consul about this!"

[ ] "This is a terrible inconvenience. I'll register with local police because I have to, but I still think they could come up with a more efficient system."

America is a nation governed by elected officials. The democratic system was established with checks and balances to maintain stability in government systems. Changes in government are nonviolent.

Americans feel that laws have leeway, but that law machinery should be inflexible. They object to getting a job or favors by using unfair influence. It is even worse for public officials to show favoritism. Government officials are expected to be honest. It is against the law for them to accept bribes.

Unfortunately, many nations have considerable problems in establishing and maintaining stable governments. Many have suffered revolutions or chronic coups d'etat. Some are controlled by dictators or military regimes, while others have problems with terrorist groups.

These factors, however, are beyond your control; avoid discussing them. Remember, many political systems are very different from your own and must contend with problems that you may not be aware of.

Your reaction might also reveal your resentment of systems that diminish your importance as an individual or seek to control your lifestyle. Americans like to think of themselves as distinct individuals. Most Americans will cooperate and compromise for the sake of action (as you surely must in this new culture); but they like to think that they are making up their own minds and being self-reliant.

However, considering the strong emphasis on competition and the importance of the individual, most Americans are amazingly conformist in their orientation. "Keeping up with the Joneses" means not only trying to improve one's lot in life, but doing so within the norms of acceptable behavior.

Case V
Social Norms

As an employee of an international company, you have been assigned indefinitely to an overseas branch. Because you are single and will not be returning to the United States for a number of years, you want to establish some social relationships with fellow employees and natives of the country.

But, many of the things you say and do are met with disapproval. For example, during the first few weeks on the job you got some odd stares as you got to know your associates. And you thought they'd appreciate being called by their first names, but some of them seemed offended. You soon realized that you can't be direct and outspoken in your criticism. You're confused about how to handle management problems if you can't approach employees in a frank, direct manner.

Even socially you're treading on thin ice. All those casual habits, perfectly acceptable at home, are simply not acceptable where you are. Like that date you had to the movies last week—she was obviously annoyed that you didn't wear a tie and suit coat, and she was shocked when you tried to hold her hand while walking down the street.

What are your feelings about these responses to your behavior?

[ ] "They don't like me because I'm an American. I wonder if they'll even give me a chance to show them what a friendly guy I really am."

[ ] "What a bunch of stuffed shirts! Don't they ever loosen up?"

[ ] "Well, if they think I'm going to let them get away with anything just because they can't take a little criticism, they're wrong!"

[ ] "What a put down. Just because I wanted to hold her hand doesn't mean I wanted to marry the girl. I guess her folks have taught her to be afraid of men."

[ ] "Looks like I'll have to do some changing myself if I want to get along with the people here."

[ ] "They really are different here. I want to learn to recognize important differences and act accordingly."

Americans are readily recognized by foreigners as the ones with the ready smile and the firm handshake. They are outgoing and have a strong public-relations orientation. Although foreigners generally admire this attitude, it also confuses them, for they consider Americans to have a very shallow idea of friendship.

America is generally a noncontact society. A kiss or embrace is used publicly as greeting or farewell only among family or very close friends. Common American social and dating practices may be considered extreme in other cultures. For example, any public display of affection, such as holding hands, can be offensive.

Americans are generally very direct in their approach to other people. "Telling it like it is" describes the face-to-face confrontations that characterize the modern American approach to interpersonal problems. Americans "meet the problem head on," "put all their cards on the table," and get it "straight from the horse's mouth." They consider being forthright and outspoken a sign of honesty. They speak frankly and directly, and do not feel that they are being unpleasant in so doing. In many other cultures, however, directness and open criticism are extremely offensive.

Most other cultures have preserved formality for first meetings, public appearances, and other social relationships. The intimacy of calling a person by his or her first name is reserved for close relationships. The informal dress of the United States can be unacceptable in other countries. How do Americans perceive formality and protocol? As pompous and arrogant? Most American men dislike wearing a tie and jacket unless it is necessary. Many Americans call everyone by their given name immediately, even on first meeting.

You may ask, if I can't be myself in another culture, what "self" can I be? What can I do and say?

Some of your personal characteristics and habits may be unacceptable in the culture you will be living in; but common courtesy and respect for the feelings of others should direct you in deciding how to act with people so that everyone is comfortable.

Most people will understand that you are new in their culture, and will accept more blunders from you than they would from another native. People are normally sympathetic to visitors who admit their limitations and seek help. Rather than being alienated by poor language ability or *faux pas,* many people come to the aid of visitors who frankly admit, "I'm just now learning your language and your customs. Please help me understand." Despite the goodwill and patience of your hosts, you owe them a wholehearted effort to learn and respect customs that are important to them.

*To **know** may not be enough;*
*to properly **do** may not suffice;*
*To **feel** may even be unimportant;*
Yet, to train others how to
*Acceptably **know**, **feel** and **do***
Builds Bridges of Understanding.
(V. Lynn Tyler)

What Would You Do?

Interpersonal communication between people whose cultures and life experiences are very different requires special skills. It's basic that you understand ways of living, communicating, and thinking of others. A working knowledge of the language in the other country will be extremely helpful. In addition, nonverbal cues may convey more to you than spoken words. Different circumstances will also alter your comprehension and expectations.

Apply helpful ideas you have learned in analyzing the preceding examples to complete the following exercise. (Add your own!)

Knowing that Americans feel like this	*And that other cultural viewpoints may be these*	*What can you do for pleasant interactions?*
1. Americans are accustomed to many things that are considered luxuries in other lands.	In many cultures you will be considered rich simply because you are an American.	Modify lifestyle to conform to circumstances and comforts.
2. Americans believe that they can create their own destiny; a person can achieve what he or she is willing to plan, sacrifice, and work for.	The people of many cultures believe that they have very little to say about what comes in life, that fate deals out what is in store for them. It is proper to accept one's fate without questioning.	Suspend judgment and be patient with necessary limitations.
3. Americans are competitive and aggressive and admire those who achieve success through hard work.	Some cultures consider it inappropriate or impossible for one to alter the social position or status into which one is born.	**You continue:**

4. Americans of all social classes engage in physical labor.

Many cultures consider manual labor demeaning.

Possible Interactions:

5. There is emphasis on looking, acting, and feeling young. The old are often cared for in nursing homes.

Wisdom comes with age, and the elderly are greatly respected and honored.

6. American families are mostly nuclear, consisting of only the parents and children.

Many families in the world are extended, consisting of several generations, including distant relatives.

7. Americans are accustomed to great freedom of choice, movement, and expression. The people can limit government control.

Many forms of government conflict with the American ideal of freedom of choice and action. Many countries have had difficulty maintaining stability in government.

8. Americans are very mobile. They think nothing of moving thousands of miles if their job requires it, and of leaving family and friends and making new friends quickly.

Many of the world's people have never traveled more than 50 miles from their places of birth. Their acquaintances are those they have known all their lives.

9. Americans consider themselves independent. They want to make their own decisions and expect and enjoy recognition for individual achievement.

The groups one identifies with may be more important than individual effort or recognition.

10. Americans are informal and usually outgoing. They call everyone by first names. Social manners are generally informal.

Most cultures preserve formality in public interaction. Public displays of affection and informality in dress can be offensive.

Possible Interactions:

11. Americans have relatively little respect for rank or authority, especially inherited authority. They think people should earn their right to rule.

Many people of the world accept their station in life willingly and seldom question those in power.

12. Americans are frank and outspoken. They consider it a sign of honesty to speak candidly.

Directness and open criticism are considered extremely offensive. Delicate negotiations are often handled by intermediaries.

What strange creatures we—thinking nothing is "real" unless others use our name for it!
(From Bonnie Lloyd, mother of a deaf child.)

How Others May See You

Initially it may be difficult for you to accept and understand how people from other countries view you, your country, and your culture. Being stereotyped can be annoying to anyone. By understanding how others perceive you as a foreigner, you can be better prepared to help them understand you, and you them.

Stereotypes can be used as starting points to determine what people are really like. The following describes how various peoples of the world view Americans:

Careless: With dress, possessions, time, money, rules, manners, ceremonies, nature, relationships, politics, and more.

Generous/Hospitable: As victors in war, as neighbors, as U.N. benefactors.

Self-indulgent: Pursuing material things.

Sentimental/Romantic: Prone to extremes in emotional expression; open.

Materialistic: Usually honest; ambition and success are paramount; vastness.

Confident and Self-Confident: Even brash, yet demand almost too much of self.

Complacent yet Arrogant: Ethnocentric, embarrassingly so; misunderstand honor.

Colonistic: Ethnocentrically imperialistic; disregard for other systems; overly proud of own systems.

Competitive yet Equalitarian: A paradox to most in children-to-adult varieties; class and rank may be temporary; no real aristocracy.

Resourceful: Combining all of the above; lovers of common sense and results, inventions, innovations, and flexibility; "now" oriented.

Independent and Different: Individually feeling not to "fit others' mold," but fiercely defensive if encroached upon as an American.

> *Stereotypes are most at folly when dealing with individuals; but they are most useful when dealing with peoples in general . . . as in this instance.*
>
> (Adapted from Wu-Kuang Chu)

If you agree with these perceptions, why do you? If not, how are Americans different from this? How can you help others understand your feelings? How can you understand theirs? Search for the keys to effective intercultural understanding in your own experiences.

Just as Americans are so much more than "pizza, tacos, apple pie, and baseball," other people are much more than you may have thought. There are ways of developing accurate perceptions and of building bridges over which you and others considerately can cross.

> *If a [person] be gracious and courteous to strangers, it shows he is a citizen of the world, and that his heart is no island cut off from other lands, but a continent that joins to them.*
>
> (Sir Francis Bacon)

Chapter 5

Questions Asked and Answers Questioned

> *What right have we to change another people by interacting with them? What right have we not to?*
>
> (Everett Kleinjens)

Realistic Responses

You will undoubtedly be asked many questions based on stereotypes about your country and culture as you cross intercultural boundaries. In our interdependent, complex world, many concerns of people of one country will be of interest to others. But such issues often raise questions that are difficult to respond to because of their many implications. You may feel offended or confused as you attempt to answer them. Your answers may evoke even more difficult questions.

Some people ask questions out of honest curiosity; others may have sincere criticism of your society. As a citizen ambassador, you should be prepared to respond appropriately and consistently to questions directed to you. By doing so you can (1) learn more about yourself culturally as a citizen of your own country, (2) provide a balanced perspective of your people's accomplishments and continuing challenges, and (3) develop skill in finding common ground that can serve as a basis for effective interaction with others.

Questions: *When they are effective, the results can be very dramatic. When they are not, the results can also be very dramatic.*

(Anonymous)

Avoid Arguments

When you're arguing, it's difficult to pay attention to the feelings of others. Leave your high school or college debate skills at home. Most people do not want to argue with you; they often consider such behavior rude and will walk away or stop a discussion. Even if you do find someone who likes an argument, remember that no one really wins; you gain little except frustration. Instead of arguing, simply say something like, "That is something I know little about," or "You may have a point. I would like to follow it up later."

Find Out What Critics are Really Thinking

Be careful to "read between the lines" for what people truly want. Only time and patience can help you find out what their real complaints are (their "hidden agenda"). Ask, "What specifically do you feel may cause people from my country to act as you think they do (or do not)?" Retorts ("You just don't understand!") are easy to deliver but do little good. Avoid cross-examinations, putting the critic's own country on the spot, or otherwise trying to trap a potential critic. Build on any positive feelings he or she may have about another aspect of your country or culture. Then, if useful, come back to the point of criticism after you have built a rapport. Sympathy usually works wonders. It rarely fails!

Draw On Your Own Experience

Agree with your critics as much as possible. Perhaps they are complaining about the violence and improprieties on television, a point you agree with. Tell how you personally feel about it and perhaps what you're trying to do about it. This way you can escape the pitfalls of dealing with generalities (such as "They're all immoral") and come to a better understanding of what the critic disapproves of.

Get the Discussion Beyond the Context of Your Own Country

Because you are the "foreigner" to other people, critics may use you as a whipping post for universal problems such as prejudice, immorality, or poverty. Rather than being specific (as suggested above), be more general. Talk about prejudice, immorality, and poverty as global problems. Point out what other people are doing or not doing about such problems, and the implications of such action. Be careful not to cite the critics' country unless they bring it up; then try to be positive about the ways people there are dealing with similar concerns.

Be Reasonable

How you respond to questions will often have more influence than what you say; courtesy is hard to argue against. Appropriate humor can also calm ruffled feelings. Be candid, especially as you discuss ideas common to you and the critic. Let him or her know what the views are in your country. Show your tolerance and knowledge of other cultures and countries by mentioning good things that are happening locally and throughout the world. This will illustrate your goodwill and broad perspective.

> *People are usually more convinced by reasons they have discovered themselves than those found by others.*
>
> (Defense Language Training Manual)

Take Each Question As If It Were Sincere

Responding to queries that seem hostile or critical is not easy. If you respond sarcastically or in a "put-down" way, you instantly cut off the channel of good communication. If you are haughty, others may return the attitude; if you are suspicious, they will probably also be suspicious. But if you are friendly, even if somewhat reserved, they will probably act friendly toward you even if they don't agree with you. Those who speak a language other than yours may not be able to convey the nonverbal expressions that often give real meaning to questions. Be careful to interpret the tone or style of questioners correctly. Take time to develop trust.

Don't Try To Fake It

If you don't feel comfortable answering a question because you are unfamiliar with the subject or limited in your experience, don't be afraid to say that you're not sure, and that you hope others will understand. Use available factual information. If your facts aren't too reliable, you can always offer to get more accurate information elsewhere.

> *Hearing is done with more than ears, feeling with more than touch.*
>
> (Source unknown)

But Don't Evade the Question

What if you tell someone that you do not discuss certain subjects, or that you do not want to, or are unable to answer a certain question? If the question is important to those who asked, they might wonder if you have anything important to share at all. Avoid the following statements because they may come across as defensive and irresponsible:

"I don't know; I don't care."
"I did not come here to talk about that."
"I do not want to rock the boat or say something that might be offensive."

Try these responses instead:

"My own impression is simply . . . "
"My experience may be limited, but it has been . . . "
"This is how I feel at this time . . . "

Many of the questions you may be asked are not only for information. They are sometimes games. The questioner may not be as interested in listening to *what* you say as in *how* you respond, and *why*.

Sources for Especially Hard Questions

Government agencies, banks, and multinational companies sometimes share material on "appropriate" answers to questions most often asked about your country. Try the U.S. State Department Office of Publications for speeches, summary statements, and basic background facts on countries and peoples. Other countries have their equivalent of the U.S. State Department or senator to whom you can write for information updates. You might also write the embassies of other countries, which could include you on their mailing lists.

But even when you get the "official" information, be careful. Most people appreciate concise responses to their questions rather than ones in stiff diplomatic or legal language that is hard to understand. Some universities even offer classes dealing with such "answers." More informal, and perhaps more informative, responses to common, difficult questions can be obtained from professors at major universities. Also, check on informal study groups. "Friends of (a country or area)," World Affairs Councils, and embassy attachés are usually helpful. They give you simple, "ready-to-use" responses that are most useful in current situations. There are no pat answers. Getting a variety of responses can help you deal with different situations and needs that arise since several opinions are usually better than one. Test responses before you trust them.

To Conclude—and Begin

By responding to questions appropriately, you can better understand what being a citizen of your country means, as well as satisfy an inquisitive stranger. These questions and answers can build bridges of understanding and positive intercultural interaction.

Half of the world's great ideas come from correct answers (information); the other half comes from posing appropriate questions. As you develop your expertise at questioning the answers to critical questions, you will become a more able people ambassador.

> *Make haste slowly. The meaning of a communication depends upon the context.*
>
> (Edward T. Hall)

(A number of these ideas are developed from *Citizen Ambassadors* by Dr. Charles T. Vetter, and from the Infogram *Questions Asked Americans*. See references at the end of this book.)

Chapter 6

Coming and Going: Absorbing Shocks of Culture and Self-Discovery

Is it possible to fit in everywhere—to be truly "international"? Can people adapt completely to other ways of life, and then "come home again" and fit right back into their own culture? It is doubtful. Each of us has attitudes, emotions, prejudices, habits, and mannerisms that are as much a part of us as the language we speak or the beliefs we accept and react to regularly. Changes in us occur as well as in others. Learning to adjust and readjust is part of life—especially with several significant intercultural skills.

Sign Language

You might think that knowing and using the language of a people ensures automatic communication with them. But remember, effective communication includes all behavior and circumstances. A knowledge of the written and spoken language in itself is insufficient. Your peace of mind and effectiveness in commmunicating depends on hundreds of signs and symbols that you are largely unaware of. These signs and cues you use to orient yourself to the situations of daily living include when and how to greet people, to eat, to get from place to place, and to talk informally with others.

When you enter a strange culture, all or most of these familiar cues are removed and this can make you feel like a fish out of water. No matter how broad-minded or full of goodwill you may be, you will be affected by having these props knocked out from under you. The mental and emotional adjustments required of those living abroad are real, but they can be positive adjustments to help you cope in new situations.

Some people find it harder to adapt than others. It helps to be aware that problems will arise, and to recognize what it is you are experiencing. Difficulty in confronting and coping with new cultural circumstances is called *culture shock*. This condition affects nearly every traveler—even experienced ones—yet millions of people have dealt with it. And you can, too.

Culture Shock

An intercultural experience is a powerful personal teacher that forces you to realize new things about others and about yourself. Indeed, the greatest *shock* may not be in dealing with a different culture, but in recognizing how your own culture has shaped you. You realize the extent of your culture's influence as you leave it and then try to reenter it smoothly.

This difficulty can also be called *role shock,* or the shock of self-discovery. Many times what is really shocking to people is not the new culture, but rather the change in roles they must assume in their personal, social, or organizational structure as it functions in new cultures or as they see themselves with new insights.

Accepting that adjustment is a challenge. Remember that it is a temporary condition and will pass as you become familiar with the culture. This is the first step toward adjustment. You may not like to believe you are experiencing emotional, mental, social, and physical stress, but it is wise to admit that it is happening. Even mild cases generally involve four phases and occur during the early part of a stay abroad and the return home.

Phase I: "How Quaint!"

The spirit of adventure carries you through the "honeymoon" phase. Generally someone will help you get settled, you will be excited about the newness of it all, and things will go well. You are comfortable as long as you can see similarities between your native culture and the new environment. Normally this phase does not last long if you remain abroad and must cope with real conditions of living in a different culture.

Phase II: "It's Just Not Like Home Was"

When the newness and excitement wear off (after a few hours or even several months), the real challenge begins. As you see and feel differences between your culture and the new one, things are not as you expected; you may begin to feel disoriented. Because language is the most common communicaton tool in any society, it offers the greatest security in personal relationships. If you do not have an adequate interpreter and cannot speak the language yourself, you will be stripped of your primary means of interaction. You will be unable to display the education and intelligence that give you status and security back home. As you are unable to respond to other people on their own level, you may feel that you are like a child again. This is frustrating.

Culture shock is a psychological and emotional reaction that manifests itself in physical and social behavior. Another sign that you are in the critical second phase of cultural adjustment is the tendency to associate with other "foreigners" and complain with them about the country and the people.

You may be overly concerned with the washing of hands and the cleanliness of drinking water, food, dishes, and bedding. As a result, you may fear physical contact with attendants or servants. You may also feel a dependence on long-term residents from your country. You may experience fits of anger over delays and other minor frustrations, or excessive fear at the possibility of being cheated, robbed, or injured. You show great concern over minor pains and irritations. Finally, in this phase your frustrations can be highlighted by a terrible longing just to be back home, to eat the foods you're accustomed to, to visit familiar places and relatives, and to talk to people who "really make sense."

This phase can also be characterized as "culture fatigue," something like battle fatigue. You simply get tired of not being home in comfortable circumstances. In spite of your ability to cope on a daily basis or in specific cases, you experience general stress.

Phase III: "It's Starting to Make Sense"

The first sign of your transition through this critical phase is the return of your unconscious sense of humor. (If you haven't lost it, the adjustment is much more rapid.) You enter the third phase when you begin to recognize communicative cues: people's facial expressions, actions, and tones. And you begin to piece together a pattern of behaving and living. Mastering a working knowledge of the language, you begin to communicate more effectively. As you increase your familiarity and knowledge, you find yourself getting through each day with greater ease.

Many government and private organizations specialize in preparing Americans to adjust to their intercultural experience. Several such programs suggest to their participants that to be adequate "culture shock absorbers," they must first develop self-awareness—an understanding of their own feelings and cultural patterns, of what offends or confuses them, and of why they feel dissatisfied. The visitors should suspend judgment about conditions they find unpleasant or confusing until they learn more about the people and the reasons these people think and act as they do. The recovery stage progresses rapidly as visitors begin to empathize with the natives of the host culture. They imaginatively meet each challenging or perplexing situation, and are concerned more with gaining new insights and friends than with feeling uncomfortable about their inadequacies or the country's seeming oddities. They remember who "the foreigner" really is. It is in this phase that real learning begins.

Phase IV: "I Understand and Enjoy"

The fourth and final phase can carry you through your stay abroad and your return home. Now that you are willingly adjusting to the new culture, you can accept it as just another way of living. It does not mean that you are enthusiastic about everything the people do or about the way they do it; it does mean that you can accept and understand the differences. You still have moments of strain and times of misunderstanding, but you begin to feel more comfortable and will genuinely enjoy yourself.

Some people take to other cultures more quickly than others. Also, you may adapt more quickly to one culture than to another. The more a culture differs from your own, the more difficult you can expect your adjustment to be. However, if you have had previous intercultural experiences, you will probably have fewer problems.

> *The greatest distance between humankind is often the last eighteen inches.*
>
> (Dwight D. Eisenhower, adapted)

Cultivating Awareness for Active Applications

You will adapt readily to other cultures to the extent that you have the following characteristics:

Awareness of and Flexibility with Self: You need a positive self-image and the ability to adapt to be emotionally stable in situations that challenge personal feelings. Self-motivation allows you to *act* positively, rather than to *react* negatively, to strange environments.

Awareness of and Flexibility with Others: A tolerance for ambiguity and uncertainty makes it easier to understand, learn from, and work with people who are from different cultures.

Awareness of and Flexibility with Circumstances: A sensitivity to circumstances allows you to pick up behavior patterns more quickly. If you look, listen, and imitate appropriately, you can communicate more effectively with people around you, and you will be able to establish pleasant relationships.

Adjusting to a new culture can be a powerful learning experience. Although you may suffer temporary frustration, discomfort, and anxiety, these feelings can help you understand yourself and develop your personality. The very experiences that disrupt your personality and your relationship to your surroundings will be the basis on which you can build an expanded and enlightened personality.

Half the battle of cultural adjustment is won if you realize you will experience it in a variety of ways: mentally, emotionally, physically, and socially. The other half is won by using your cultural sensitivity to learn and to make positive adjustments. Once you realize that many of your problems are caused by your inability to comfortably accept another's cultural background, you can gain an understanding, learn to communicate, and more readily enjoy your experience.

What Would You Do?

Below are examples of some situations you might encounter while in a different culture. Considering the discussion on absorbing culture shock, decide what reaction you might have in each situation. You may want to determine what reaction would be appropriate in a specific culture, e.g., Brazilian, Japanese, or German, etc. Note your reasons—the "why" for each choice.

1. *You take a shoe to the repair shop to get resoled with leather. The repairman promises to have it done the next day. When you return the leather hasn't even been tanned yet; your shoe hasn't been mended. The repairman promises to have it done that afternoon.*

[ ] You ask when you can check back to get the shoe.

[ ] Angrily, you demand that he explain why he didn't keep his promise.

[ ] You tell him you'll be back at three and that if the job isn't done, you'll take your shoe elsewhere.

[ ] You tell him that where you come from, people are more efficient and keep their promises.

2. *You are alone for an afternoon and decide to visit some downtown stores. After you've had your fill of book, gift, and clothing shops, you want to return home. You don't know the language, and you have no idea where to catch the bus.*

[ ] You find a friendly-looking man and try to ask for his help using elaborate, spontaneous sign language.

[ ] You try to ask some shopkeepers if they can direct you to someone who speaks English.

[ ] You decide to walk a few blocks and see if you happen to pass a bus stop.

[ ] You start looking for a road map.

3. *At a social gathering you are introduced to a friend of the host. He is eager to practice speaking your language and engages you in a conversation about your country's national elections. All the while he is standing very close to you, squeezing your arm and fingering your lapel like he wants to buy your coat.*

[ ] You patiently hold your ground and pleasantly answer his questions.

[ ] You back away so that he cannot touch you and continue the conversation at a comfortable distance.

[ ] You find a reason to excuse yourself and manage to avoid him for the rest of the evening.

[ ] You slip him a breath mint and tell him to keep his hands to himself.

4. *One sweltering afternoon you go to the kitchen to fix lunch. Several biscuits were left out on the table that morning, much to the delight of some large, hungry, scary-looking bugs that scurry to safety as you enter the room.*

[ ] You scream, slam the door, and refuse to enter again until the kitchen is fumigated.

[ ] You ask your neighbor for advice about how to store food properly so that it will not attract bugs or rodents (which are even scarier).

[ ] You move to a "cleaner" apartment.

[ ] You decide to ignore the poor etiquette of your multi-legged friends who rudely eat and run.

5. *You are thirsty and your hostess brings you a glass of ice water. You have been warned about drinking untreated water in this country.*

[ ] You tell her that you're really not thirsty after all.

[ ] You thank her and drink the water, hoping you'll be lucky.

[ ] You ask her if the water has been boiled.

[ ] You drink it, teeth closed, hoping the water will be strained of harmful bacteria.

6. *You visit the busy outdoor market, though you don't intend to buy anything. The vendors are advertising their wares loudly, but some also grab your sleeve and step in front of you to prevent your passing.*

[ ] You fight your way away from the vendors, leaving the market as soon as possible.

[ ] You observe how other people are turning down the insistent salesmen. Using these techniques, you continue to browse through the market.

[ ] You angrily push the vendors aside, getting in an elbow now and then for good measure.

[ ] You consider screaming the word for *fire* until everyone clears out of your way.

7. *When you are introduced to a man, he says, "You must come dine with us sometime."*

[ ] You say, "Thank you" and continue the conversation, knowing that his invitation was merely a formality.

[ ] You make an appointment to dine with the family.

[ ] You ignore his invitation and continue the conversation.

[ ] You decline because you aren't sure of the proper response to a dinner invitation.

8. *You visit a host family for the first time. The entire family is present, and all are smiling and obviously pleased to meet you. However, only the male adults extend their hands as you approach them.*

[ ] You shake hands with the male adults only.

[ ] You shake hands with all the adults and the children.

[ ] You shake hands with the male adults and look for a sign from them about whether the women and children should be approached.

[ ] You ignore the women and children completely.

9. *You are a speaker at a public meeting. As another man addresses the audience, you begin to feel tired and stiff. You want very much to stretch your arms and relieve your legs by crossing them.*

[ ] You wait until the speaker is finished, then stretch your arms and legs.

[ ] You don't stretch, but you do cross your legs.

[ ] You fold your arms and look cross.

[ ] You resist stretching and crossing your legs.

10. *Most of your co-workers, natives of the culture, give you disapproving looks as you leave work to go home while they prepare to play ball together for a few hours before leaving.*

[ ] You take off your coat and play with them.

[ ] You evade their glances and leave as quickly as possible.

[ ] You explain to some of those standing nearby that you have an appointment; then you hurry out.

11. *You take your child to a school to enroll him. The door guard, however, will not allow you to enter the building to see the headmaster.*

[ ] You assure him you are there only to see the headmaster and beg him to let you pass.

[ ] You threaten to report him if he doesn't let you in.

[ ] You ask a local friend how you can gain access to the headmaster.

[ ] You go look for another school.

12. *Some workers under your supervision are late in completing their work and are not doing it properly.*

[ ] You call the worst offenders to your office, confront them with the problem, and tell them they will be fired if they do not shape up.

[ ] You explain the problem to the workers and let them know you expect each one to fulfill his or her work obligations.

[ ] You don't do anything.

[ ] You intimate to some of your workers that you are displeased with the work, hoping that this will eventually get back to the offenders.

13. *You are unfamiliar with the native currency. In a store you indicate the item you wish to buy. You ask the clerk how much it costs, but you do not understand his response.*

[ ] You try to communicate with "sign language."

[ ] You hold out some money and motion for the clerk to take the price of the item.

[ ] You try to locate someone who speaks English to help you.

[ ] You go elsewhere, hoping to find a store with a clerk who speaks English.

14. *As you enter a home, you begin to remove your shoes, but your host insists it is not necessary for you to do so.*

[ ] You remove your shoes anyway.

[ ] You leave your shoes on.

[ ] You take one off and leave the other on.

15. *An acquaintance gives you a wrapped gift as he enters your home.*

[ ] You unwrap the gift immmediately.

[ ] You wait for the guest to invite you to unwrap it.

[ ] You wait until he leaves to unwrap the gift.

16. *You are a passenger on a crowded bus. You have to get off at the next stop. You signal the bus driver, and he slows down but doesn't stop.*

[ ] You are puzzled and decide to watch other people getting off the bus to see how they signal the bus driver to stop.

[ ] You take a leap from the bus as it slows.

[ ] You become angry and yell at the bus driver to stop.

17. *You have invited a local family to your home for dinner. The meal is ready by 8:00, but your guests don't arrive until 9:30.*

[ ] You don't comment, but serve your guests the overcooked food.

[ ] You tell your guests how rude they are for arriving late.

[ ] You tell them you ruined the meal and you're very sorry.

[ ] You suggest that you all go out to a restaurant.

18. *Walking on the street, you are approached by a child who is poorly dressed and looks miserable and hungry. He extends his hand and begs for money.*

[ ] You press a coin into his hand and wish him a good day.

[ ] You push him aside and tell him you have no money to give him.

[ ] You ignore him completely.

19. *You ask directions haltingly in a foreign language; following the directions, you arrive at the wrong place.*

[ ] You decide that from now on, it would be wise to consult two or three people for directions.

[ ] You assume you asked the questions incorrectly or you misunderstood the man's reply.

[ ] You decide to ask directions only from those who can speak English.

Go back and consider each choice you made. Is there a better choice, perhaps, that is not listed? Think of the best way to deal with each situation. Following are some comments that frequently indicate that the speaker is experiencing culture shock. What point of view could you take instead?

1. "How about cleaning this place?"

_____

2. "Are they ever on time?"

_____

3. "It's really different from home."

4. "I've never seen so many poor people."

5. "My friends back home will never believe that . . ."

6. "I can hardly wait to get back home so I can . . ."

> *Against the assault of laughter, nothing can stand.*
> (Mark Twain)

Absorbing Return Shock

We have intimated that going home after visiting other countries is often a difficult change for some people. Get ready for "reverse cultural shock" when you return home! The changes back home or your new perceptions that come from being away may not come as a surprise. Shock is common whenever you encounter a dramatic change, whether it involves employment, housing, marital status, or moving. Even the natural changes in growing from childhood to adolescence to adulthood produce emotional, social, and physical shock. All forms of shock require an adjustment period.

The reassuring aspect of change is that it produces internal growth if handled correctly. Your intercultural interactions will be with those who have changed, just as you have.

You've Changed Inside . . .

Your insights will have broadened and your perspectives will be different. Be aware that your emotional and mental climates have also changed. An attempt at an immediate reversion to "the old you" will likely fail. Hopefully the internal changes have been positive ones and there is no need for a reversion. Temper your desires to convert those around you. They may not be willing or able to understand the changes that have occurred in you. It will depend, of course, on how long you have been away; also they may not be interested in the "new you" and your attitudes toward the world, your desire to "improve things" or even to go back to the "good old ways."

One seasoned traveler says diplomacy is the key. If you were wildly enthusiastic about your foreign country, it's best not to say so if your family and friends want to hear how relieved you are to be back on the home turf. It's not unusual to find that they consider you slightly disloyal for having left at all, and far more so for having enjoyed it to the hilt.

. . . And Out

Realize that you have changed culturally. (So have others, for that matter. Their experiences will have changed them while you've been away.) You have become Europeanized (or some other- - "ized") after an extended stay away from home. It may be difficult to fit back into your former lifestyle without some struggling. The healthiest solution to this dilemma might be to combine the positive aspects of the old and the new. The result is a much richer and enjoyable lifestyle.

It is probably unwise to impose your cultural changes on friends and family. They might not appreciate being told the "proper way to eat," the "civilized way to address others," or other "better" ways to do things. Vent your frustrations in the supportive atmosphere of others like yourself who have also been abroad.

> *How you fix lunch affects how you communicate. Knowing how is as important as knowing why.*
>
> (Source unknown)

Mild Surprise or Mega-Shock

The degree of shock experienced by each traveler can range from a mild jolt to uncomfortable agitation. The experienced traveler with a multinational personality probably suffers minimal return shock, while the novice might need an extensive readjustment period.

There are a number of factors that determine how great or small your adjustment may be:

1. The length of time you've been away.

2. Whether or not you've been to that particular place before.

3. How much contact with home you maintained while you were away.

4. How often you have traveled before. (A word of caution: Success in one return experience doesn't necessarily guarantee you will be successful the next time, and vice versa.)

5. Whether or not your time away was enjoyable.

6. Who traveled with you. Whether you traveled alone or with family or friends are factors that can influence your return home experiences.

Advice to the Prepared

Expect Differences

Unexpected changes in life are harder to deal with than expected changes. Generally, the more unexpected the change, the more stress it causes. Use change as a tool, not a foe—as a teacher rather than a taskmaster.

Guard Your Health

Expect some exhaustion, depression, or anxiety, which often accompany long-distance travel and return-home stress. The condition is temporary, especially when you know what to expect and how to cope. (*Taming Travel Stress,* an Infogram published by the Brigham Young University David M. Kennedy Center for International Studies, discusses effects of jet lag and other travel stress.)

Getting it Back Together

Identify your new options as soon as possible after arriving home (after prearranging as much as possible). Make plans for developing a lifestyle that combines the best of the old and the new. Making long-term goals will motivate you in your work, enhance your family life, and strengthen you and your friendships.

Be proud of your new international status and start thinking about your next experience in another culture!

In the Beginning . . .

The best time to prepare to come home again is before you leave. Your interactions away from home become part of you, and people at home also develop different perspectives while you are away. Consider intercultural interactions to be an opportunity to increase your self-discovery, and you'll be ready to absorb the stress, and indeed to become a global citizen.

Chapter 7

Selecting Sensitive Symbols
of Respect

> *Cultural imperialism is to rob others of their identity.*
>
> (Source Unknown)

Intercultural interaction often breeds anxiety about protocol, especially in terms of showing respect to others. How many times have you asked yourself, even when you were in familiar settings, "Should I tip?" "To whom should I give special respect?" "How important is it that I call others by their official title?" "What type of gift would be appropriate to show that I really do appreciate them?" A good rule of thumb in dealing with such questions is to investigate before you invest.

Selecting symbols of respect is essential to good interaction, for such symbols are nonverbal communication. Each symbol—a bow, a tip, or a gift—sends a message to the recipient, who will interpret it favorably or unfavorably. But how much depends on their culture, the symbol given, and the way it is given? Some general guidelines can help you determine when something is appropriate, and when it is not. Test these guidelines now so that you can trust them later.

> *Your world and mine may be very different, but in one way they are alike: both affect the way we communicate, or do not. Those who bring sunshine into the lives of others cannot keep it from themselves.*
>
> (Source Unknown)

Thoughtfulness

Any symbol of respect—kind words, and especially a gift—is more valuable when given with more thought than money. Giving respect by giving of yourself is essential to intercultural protocol. Giving a gift that is well thought out and sincere helps the receiver see you as a unique person, rather than as an acquaintance who is only going through the motions.

Studying

As with any effort at interaction, you should learn local customs so that you can be sensitive to both verbal and nonverbal communication in that culture. For instance, some Europeans still practice a traditional chivalry that may seem outdated, even humorous.

Conversation

Determine which topics of and approaches to conversation are appropriate and which are not. Giving a token of respect will not be appreciated if your conversation deals with an issue that is generally not brought up among short-term acquaintances—personal habits, for example.

Reciprocity

Having given a gift or symbol of respect, allow the recipient to reciprocate. Otherwise you may place the receiver in an inferior position and appear superior because of your generosity. For many, especially Americans who tend to think of themselves as independent, receiving a gift or symbol of respect is difficult. It may be "more blessed to give than to recieve," but if you are not a willing and courteous receiver, your giving can be inappropriate.

> *The language of influence is that most often misperceived.*
>
> (Source Unknown)

Meaning

What does a title, a courtesy, or a gift mean to the recipient? It may be seen as a symbol of regard—or perhaps as a bribe. You must identify your motive for giving the symbol. Remember that giving a gift or token of esteem almost always incurs obligation, and the receiver will want to reciprocate somehow.

Gift Giving: A Case Study

Giving a gift is often an acceptable way to show your respect and admiration for another person or group of people. Each culture has its customs about what is considered appropriate. Let's take Japan as an example of a culture with unique gift-giving customs. Below are some types of "gifting" in Japan, adapted from *Do's and Taboo's Around the World,* edited by Roger E. Axtell and compiled by The Parker Pen Company (Wiley Press, New York, 1985). Be sure to *test* before you *trust.* You will need specific directions from people "in the know."

1. An excessive show of gratitude for a gift should not be expected. The Japanese recipient may not even open it in front of you.

2. Let your counterpart initiate the gift exchange unless he or she is visiting you.

3. When giving a return gift, don't worry about it reflecting the same monetary value, size, or even uniqueness of the gift you received. Thoughtfulness is much more important.

4. Be patient. Find the right time and place to show appreciation and respect. Do not be pushy. Avoid singling out individuals, who may be embarrassed by a public display of recognition or gratitude. Be careful with surprises. It is better to subtly inquire about what is or is not expected.

5. Choose food, colors, size, type (be careful with animals or their representations), and value according to advice from those who know what is appropriate. Be very cautious with thank-you cards, flowers, liquor, clothing, and cash—or other symbols that might be viewed as showy.

People from other countries may have customs of gift giving similar to those in Japan. But even if they don't, many of the guidelines above can apply to the culture you are concerned with. Be especially careful to check on the wording you will use to go along with gifts or other symbols of respect.

Respect Through Tipping

Tipping is a source of anxiety for the visitor to another culture or country because customs vary widely. For example, in some Asian countries you don't tip taxi drivers. In mainland China, tipping is illegal. Icelanders consider any tipping an insult, while in France and the United States, a tip is expected for almost any service rendered. Tips on tipping include these:

1. Check to see if a service charge has—or has not—been added to your bill. You needn't pay twice.

2. Extra service requires adding to the tip. Otherwise give the normal amount for that country or circumstance.

3. Leave a smaller tip if you are displeased with the service. You will show that you haven't forgotten to tip, but are not pleased with the service.

4. Offer tips to people you take pictures of. In some countries, particularly those who use bartering, small gifts (pens, costume jewelry, etc.) are more appropriate than a tip.

5. Make a practice of tipping the maid who tends your room. She is usually poorly paid and often forgotten.

6. Above all, don't hesitate to ask those around you what is normal for tipping procedures. Customs differ, so don't be

embarrassed to ask. Normally, a tip is ten to fifteen percent of your bill, but ask others to make sure.

What other symbols of respect are there besides gift giving and tipping? We have already mentioned bowing and using titles in addressing others. Consider also that punctuality, use of first and last names, and discretion in where you sit so as to maintain your status all show respect and, in turn, caring for others.

A Checklist (To Use When in Doubt)

1. How is this symbol a compliment or tribute? (Is it lavish or insufficient?)

2. In what ways are different relationships implied: business, friendship, concern?

3. To whom is the symbol of respect offered?
   a. Associate
   b. Child
   c. Spouse
   d. Other

4. When is an indirect show of respect (through an intermediary in private) more acceptable than a direct or personal approach?

5. Will the receiver see the symbol as something he can reciprocate? How?

6. If there has been an apparent gaffe or mistake, when is it best to make it right? (Immediately? Privately?)

7. What is legal; what is not?

You will need to seek help to determine the specifics of each situation by studying local customs, determining what the symbols are, and using them sensitively when acceptable to show your appreciation and respect.

> *The risks of not facing intercultural problems squarely are too great to take.*
>
> (Wilbur T. Blume)

Chapter 8

Using, Not Abusing, Those "In the Middle"— Interpreters/Translators

> *Ultimately, what makes sense (or not) is irrevocably culturally determined and depends heavily on the context in which the evaluation is made. The result is that people in culture-contact situations frequently fail to really understand each other.*
>
> (Edward T. Hall)

Will your interactions with people of another culture require the use of an interpreter or translator? Even if you know the language, you may need assistance in understanding what is being said or written. Using "the person in the middle" properly will enhance your interaction with peoples of other cultures. On the other hand, misusing this important resource can have serious consequences. Special skills are required to be an effective interpreter or translator. Equally important skills are needed to use these resource people effectively. Interpreters speak for you; translators write for you. We will explore the use of both.

When you have a message for an audience, your interpreters are in a precarious position—the middle. It is their challenge to convey your message so that your audience understands it as *you* want it to be. And that means far more than just putting words into another language.

It is possible for a person to understand the words but not the meaning, because emotions, patterns of thinking, and certain interactions vary between cultures. The interpreter must phrase the message in such a way that meanings remain intact. Effective use of an interpreter requires rapport between (1) you and your interpreter, (2) you and your audience, and (3) your interpreter and your audience. This three-way communication complicates the already delicate process of interaction.

The process by which one interprets is also more complex than we might expect. Consider the following illustration of an interpreter's challenge:

Speaker Says	*Interpreter*
Phrase 1	Listens to phrase 1.
Phrase 2	States phrase 1 in new language setting.
	Listens to own re-creation of phrase 1.
	Hears phrase 2.
Phrase 3	Remembers meaning and impact of phrase 1.
	Hears phrase 3.
	. . . and so on, anticipating feedback, innovative logic, and other changes.

Guidelines can help you help those in the middle with their seemingly impossible task so that they can help your audience (be it one or many people) understand your message, and you theirs. The following are suggestions for formal use of interpreters. Situations and interaction needs will vary, but you should never abuse your interpreter.

> *Language, like a map, is frequently used to equate people, things, places, and events that may actually be quite different. It does propose directions, but only with limited information which becomes useful only as dimensions of the map can be applied in a culturally realistic manner to real situations.*
>
> (Adapted from Seymour Fersh)

Working Effectively with Interpreters

Before Meeting Your Interpreter

1. *Survey the situation.* Learn as much as you can about the event(s). Where will it be, and who will be there? How long will you be expected to speak? Does this include time for interpretation? (Consecutive interpreting at least doubles your speaking time. If you are asked to speak for an hour, allow one-half of that time for the translation, unless you are sure that simultaneous translation is available and feasible.)

2. *Organize your message and make a list of difficult phrases.* Organize your message into thought units as much as possible. List the words, phrases, and illustrations that might give an interpreter difficulty (e.g., technical terms, familiar expressions that are hard to understand for those who have learned your language primarily from printed matter). If possible, have these phrases translated before the presentation and give or send the translation to the interpreter.

Be sure your development of ideas is straightforward without flashbacks, parenthetical additions, or footnote references. Examples should be positive, unambiguous, and as universal as possible. Avoid wordplay (e.g., "Plan your work; work your plan."); if you cannot, be sure to explain your meaning and give clear examples. Allusions cause confusion. Check feedback carefully.

3. *Review your message,* if possible, with someone who speaks the host language. They may be able to tell you which passages will be difficult to interpret accurately.

4. *Be careful in using jokes or humorous experiences.* What is humorous in your own culture may be offensive or simply not funny in the host culture. Ask others from the host culture what topics and examples can be humorous. Be careful not to take risks on topics that are controversial or offensive. Again: test before trust!

5. *Learn significant words, phrases, and quotations.* Learn greetings and colloquial terms that are appropriate for your audience. Find out when and where these can be used most effectively. Be aware that your use of a few phrases may give the impression that you know more than you do. So be prepared to say something that indicates the limit of your skills in the host language, such as, "That's the limit of my present knowledge, but I hope to learn more." People who know the culture and language or who will coordinate your visit can help you learn such phrases.

6. *Translate quotes and captions beforehand.* Whenever possible, use quotes and other references, captions for visual aids, or other resource materials that have been translated previously. A translation service may be able to provide these for you if you allow sufficient time. Otherwise, you will want to send the interpreter copies of these materials before your presentation. Plan to have material for people to read in their own language, as appropriate.

7. *Send the interpreter a copy of your presentation* ahead of time if possible. Include visuals and perhaps a list of questions you expect your listeners to ask with your tentative answers.

8. *Practice delivering your message,* so that sentences are clear and meaningfully paced (not too fast or too slow, and not as if they were being read). Eliminate "uh's" and unnecessary interjections, such as "you know," "et cetera," "and so forth."

9. *Practice with a stand-in interpreter.* If possible have a speaker of the host language react to a practice presentation of your message. Or get a friend or member of your family to act as your practice interpreter, paraphrasing your message into simple English. This

can give you some idea of potential problems in conveying your ideas in another language.

10. *Observe others who are using interpreters.* See what you could use naturally. Able interpreters can help you in this worthwhile study.

Getting to Know Your Interpreter

1. *Determine your interpreter's method.* What method does your interpreter use? Ask! Interpreters vary in experience, language background, and method preference. If possible, work for at least a few minutes with the interpreter before the actual presentation.

2. *Adjust your presentation to the interpreter's method.* Inexperienced interpreters tend to translate almost word for word Keep your presentation simple. Speak in brief sentences, using a minimum of words to express complete thoughts. Avoid using many adjectives, parenthetical statements, compound phrases, or vague references to other ideas.

Experienced interpreters will probably want to interpret complete thoughts. You should plan to speak in short thought groups or paragraphs. Let the interpreter translate one thought before you proceed to the next. Avoid using flowery terms and phrases, long quotations, extensive outlines, or more than two points at a time.

Very able interpreters are often asked to translate simultaneously, speaking at the same time you do. You should speak in a natural voice and at a moderate rate. You do not want to rush or drown out the interpreter. Give your thoughts as freely as possible without letting the interpreter's speaking bother you. You need to remain the message originator.

3. *Prearrange signals to use.* Decide with the interpreter what signs will indicate that you are going too fast or too slow, or that the audience does not understand. Your signs might consist of unobtrusive hand signals or cards with the words, "Too fast," "Too slow," and "Not understood" placed where the interpreter can point to them unobtrusively.

4. *Extend freedom to the interpreter to interject.* Give the interpreter freedom to interject explanations or clarification of terms or visual aids.

5. *Show appropriate appreciation to your interpreter.* In some cultures or language areas, it may be embarrassing to be thanked in public. In others an interpreter would lose face if not thanked publicly. Find out the appropriate way and place to show your appreciation. A third person from the culture can help you determine what to do. You may want to express appreciation simply as you conclude your presentation, if appropriate. If this is something that should be avoided, thank your interpreter in private.

Working With Your Interpreter

1. *Relax.* (Or at least try to seem unruffled.) This is a key to effective communication. Usually you will be speaking to friends or associates who are eager to hear what you have to say. Your interpreter makes it possible for you to convey your message.

2. *Speak to the audience rather than to the interpreter.* Speak slowly (but normally), distinctly, and directly.

3. *Allow the interpreter more access to the microphone* than you have if only one is available. Too much back-and-forth use of a microphone can distract from your message.

4. *Be sure your interpreter can see your lips, facial expressions, body movements, and all visual aids.* Frequently these convey more than your words. Different cultures use different modes to express ideas. Allow your interpreter freedom to use these.

5. *Watch the interpreter out of the corner of your eye.* Looking directly at your interpreter may make him or her nervous or embarrassed. If you notice a puzzled expression or if a prearrranged signal is used, rephrase what you are saying in simpler terms.

6. *Never ask an interpreter if you are being understood.* Avoid looking at the interpreter as if to say, "What is the problem?" Use a prearranged signal. Respect the interpreter enough to avoid embarrassment. If you did not have time to prearrange signals, it is better that you restate or rephrase your thought than that you risk embarrassing an interpreter with direct questions.

7. *If your interpreter asks you a question, answer it as simply as possible.* Use simple words and brief explanations. You may look briefly at the interpreter when answering or clarifying a

question. However, avoid smiling or nodding affirmatively, as this may be interpreted as being condescending. Return as quickly as possible to your presentation. If questions from your interpreter are frequent, you are probably being too vague or are trying to deliver too complicated a message.

8. *Give your interpreter a chance to explain visual aids:* Avoid interrupting the interpreter. Under the same circumstances, you would not want to be interrupted. A prearranged signal (a slight nod or other gesture) can indicate readiness to move on.

After Delivering Your Message

1. *Follow up with your interpreter.* Take a few moments with the interpreter, preferably in private, to determine what in your presentation seemed most helpful and what was the greatest challenge.

2. *Take notes to make your next experience easier.* These notes can be shared with others who use the interpreter or who follow you into the cultural or language area. Be sure that you record the translation accurately.

Use a form like the one below as you approach your experience with an interpreter. Note the things you should *do* in each circumstance listed below before, during, and after you deliver your message.

Summary to Working with Interpreters

Before Meeting the Interpreter

1. Survey the situation.
2. Organize thought groups and difficult phrases.
3. Note appropriate humor.
4. Avoid colloquial terms/quotations.
5. Translate quotations and captions.
6. Send the interpreter a copy of your presentation.
7. Practice.
8. Practice with a stand-in interpreter.

9. Observe others.

Getting to Know the Interpreter

1. Determine interpreter's method.
2. Adjust presentation.
3. Prearrange signals.
4. Allow interpreter to explain when necessary.
5. Show appropriate appreciation.
6. Review "work with interpreter."

After Delivering Message

1. Evaluate, with the interpreter, the effect of the message.
2. Take notes.
3. Develop a list of terms, phrases, and quotations.

Working Effectively with Translators and Translations

Travelers normally use interpreters more than they use translators. But to have messages you send ahead received with proper understanding, or to produce written texts, you need an effective translator.

The following guidelines deal primarily with printed or written messages, and are formulated as questions for you to deal with. Answers will suggest how successful you are in using the "person in the middle"—the translator.

[ ] How well does the translation achieve the same *purpose* as the original text? If changes are necessary, do they help or hinder the message? Why? A simple rule is: Make the foreign seem familiar.

[ ] How much can you depend on accuracy in translation? There are translators who claim they can translate "anything." Impossible. We all have our limitations. A simple rule is: Test the translation before you trust it.

[ ] Should you stay with a "good" translator (who has done an accurate job before)? Yes, if the job is similar. Needs can vary however. We may know what something says without knowing what it means, but the translator must be able to know meanings for

given situations. A simple rule is: Use the translator who knows his or her own language best, then your language second, but always, always, have the translation checked for accuracy and acceptability for the situation in which it will be used!

[ ] How many steps must a translation go through? Those that demand the most effective message transfer need more steps. Time is not always available. Money may not be available to provide for many steps. A *preediting* by someone familiar with both languages and cultures is desirable. When the translation is completed, a more experienced person should review the manuscript for acceptability. A simple rule is: "Cheap" can be costly—depending on the impact of the message to be conveyed (e.g., documents not only have to be exact, but also must fit the requirements of the countries in which they are to be used).

[ ] What specifications are required for the "best" translation? You can expect translators to know only so much, and the message to fit only to a degree in the transfer between languages and cultures. Ideas and nuances must be transferable, or considerable explanation may be needed—as with ad copy, abbreviated presentations, or unique systems in your country. A simple rule is: Communicate, communicate, communicate until meanings are clear.

[ ] Why handle translations all at once, if possible? If materials are to be used in several languages, each translation team need not do the conversion—for example, of metric equivalencies, of definition of vague terms, or of illustrations. Adapt messages so they will have widespread use. This not only saves cost but reduces the potential for error. A simple rule is: Use a multilanguage, experienced expert to preview material before it goes to several translators of different langauges. When possible, translators should be allowed to consult with the adapter/previewer to clarify differences.

[ ] In what ways can output style vary? Each language has its own elegance, which may not be appreciated elsewhere. Each people group has predilections. The message and its impact are more important than the words of original manuscripts. Allow for adaptations in the style of presentation to fit the audience. When several countries are getting the same presentation in the "same language," watch for cultural variations, e.g., Spanish is quite different from Mexico to Argentina to Spain (even as English is for

the Bronx, Singapore, and England!). A simple rule is: Deal with similarities, but allow for difference.

[ ] When is time of "the essence"? Forcing translators to hurry may be penny-wise but pound-foolish! Creative translation takes more time and research than original writing. Consider your intended audience. Weigh the consequences of potential miscommunication. Think through what will happen if the message is not acceptable, even though translated correctly. Two months is not too long to allow an effective translator to preview, transfer, and verify 50 to 100 pages. Also count printing, distribution and reflection time, as needed. The time will depend on the complexity of the message to be conveyed in the new language. A simple rule is: The more different the second language is from the original language, the more time you should allow for the translation to be adequately processed. Cost is relative in terms of expected outcome!

[ ] What happens when simplicity becomes complexity? What seems easy to understand in your own language can be incomprehensible for readers of translations. International business blunders have been terribly costly, let alone those incidents involving loss of friendship and respect because of miscommunication. Verify that the message will not only be understood but also *useful* to those who read it. Taste, style, cost, and other factors are as important as the language. "Everybody" may use your ideas in your own language, but it can be difficult for these ideas to fit new cultural circumstances. A simple rule is: Be sure *simple equals simple* in situations requiring translation.

[ ] How do you have it said as *they* (the audience) would say it? Sometimes it is more profitable to use fewer words, simpler illustrations, and more examples. Translations sometimes only rehash original language instead of presenting bright new packages of communication. "Dynamic equivalence" is a current description of an appropriate translation. A simple rule is: Check out readers to be sure they are prepared to use what is translated rather than being confused about why they have to read a translation. Simplify, simplify, simplify.

Most large communities have qualified translators for common languages. For less common languages, universities can often point out specialists. Again: Test the translation before you trust it.

A competent interpreter or translator will usually have this profile:

1. Integrity is essential. They will not accept assignments beyond their experience or ability. They may willingly increase their skill under your direction, but will freely admit what they cannot do well. They have the latest dictionaries and constantly read news and other material pertinent to the target language culture.

2. Deadlines are met unless delays are specified well ahead of time with just cause.

3. The upgraded manuscript or message has the desired impact in the new language setting—but always with the approval of the originator.

4. Exaggeration concerning the acceptability of the message transfer is avoided. Instead, weaknesses are pointed out so that adjustments can be made.

5. Interpreters and translators are willing to accept criticism from others to enable the message to be presented in the best form. Protecting one's own work is not the goal, but sharing the message in the best way is! As time and cost allow, the message transferrers are expected to verify their work with colleagues, particularly when there may be doubt as to appropriateness.

6. The laborer is worthy of his hire. Underbidding other translators or interpreters can be a sign of poor quality. Be careful to get the best for your investment. Cheapness, we have said, is often too costly in many ways!

> *A translation is no translation . . .*
> *unless it gives you the music of a*
> *poem along with the words.*
> (John M. Synge)

There are many dilemmas that interpreters, translators, and those who work with them face. These guidelines should be considered only as starting points for those who deal often with "those in the middle." Using interpreters' and translators' skills adequately without abusing the privilege is worthy of fair pay. Your experience in the intercultural interaction for which their service may be required can be positive or negative, depending on the performance of those who represent you and transfer your messages.

> *If we would communicate across cultural barriers, we must learn what to say and how to say it in terms of the expectations and predispositions of those to whom we want to respond.*
>
> (From Robert T. Oliver)

Chapter 9

Arranged Encounters—
A Review

Since your reasons for interacting with individuals differ from person to person, a careful study of protocol and motives can help you in every intercultural encounter. Are you a leader, teacher, or counselor in business, government, religion, professional services, or the private sector? This section should help prepare you to interact successfully with people on an individual basis.

The purpose of intercultural meetings can be to elicit information, instruct, share, counsel, interview, or motivate response. Complex communication processes are involved, especially when encounters are intimate.

Studies have shown that only about five to ten percent of usual face-to-face communication depends on the words used. Approximately one-third comes from how the voice is or is not used. Over one-half is communicated by facial expressions, body movements, and other communication codes. Assumptions about the communicators and the circumstances of the interaction may also affect the communication.

Intercultural encounters obviously require a different degree of sensitivity than encounters involving similar cultures. In every culture, certain feelings or assumptions influence how a member of that culture acts, and determine what roles they assume and what values they place on certain things events and ideas. We repeat, these feelings and assumptions are not right or wrong, not better or worse; they are just different.

The purpose of the following guidelines is to help you deal with interpersonal differences in arranged intercultural encounters. Your "style" may or may not be effective in an intercultural setting. As you anticipate an encounter, your challenge is to familiarize yourself with the ways of the people in the other culture, so that you can enhance, not hinder communication.

In each of the following situations every answer can be correct. It depends on the culture.

1. *When greeting someone, a person would*
   a. bow.
   b. shake hands.
   c. embrace.
   d. do something other than a, b, or c.
   e. do nothing special.

2. *Conversation is best conducted*
   a. from behind a desk or table.
   b. from across the room (but with no desk).
   c. with participants next to each other.
   d. without regard to seating arrangements.
   e. in a way not known to this reader.

3. *Conversational distance is generally*
   a. 3-12 inches.
   b. 12-18 inches.
   c. 18-36 inches.
   d. irrelevant.

4. *To establish rapport, you should ask questions about*
   a. family or work.
   b. political or religious beliefs.
   c. interests or hobbies.
   d. the purpose that brought you together—and none of the above.

5. *Shaking the head from side to side means*
   a. yes.
   b. no.
   c. nothing.
   d. that someone is sleepy.

6. *If participants in an encounter sit quietly with heads bowed and hands in their laps, your assumption would be that they*
   a. lack interest or are uncooperative.
   b. fear you.
   c. respect you.
   d. are confused.

7. *A person who receives a commendation for excellent personal performance should feel*
   a. that they have received a compliment, an incentive to continue excelling.
   b. offended, because group identification is more important than individual recognition.
   c. embarrassed, because they are not used to being complimented.
   d. confused, unable to respond.

> *Humanistic culture learning is based on the high probability that human beings of different cultures may have much to learn from other human beings, as well as much about them.*
>
> (Anonymous)

Why Should You Be Concerned?

All individuals in a communicative encounter must accept some cultural differences, but you carry extra responsibility. If you are in an influential position, you can set the mood for the encounter and subsequent relationship. The initiative for implementing necessary adjustments in behavior begins with the leader. As the follower or peer feels accepted and understood, reactions and reponses will be more meaningful.

Why Are You Having the Encounter?

Now that you have focused on the need for increased reponsibility, awareness, and ability in intercultural encounters, you should determine the reasons (there may be one or several) for a specific encounter. They can be be any of these:
1.   to work out a compromise when goals differ.
2.   to combine knowledge and skills to solve a difficult problem.

3. to discuss a controversial issue that may affect organizational stability.
4. to guide a person toward solving a problem.
5. to express anxiety about a personal crisis.
6. to work for a common goal, with one person directing the other.
7. to determine worthiness or capability for assignment.
8. to reprimand for serious error.
9. to have a brief exchange about some minor technical detail.
10. to elicit information necessary for making a decision or solving a problem.
11. to gain positive support for a decision or position.
12. to explore the unknown.

The objective of the encounter will usually determine the best approach to use in each culture.

What Variables Should Be Considered Before or As the Encounter Takes Place?

Be aware of and, if necessary, adjust to the following variables which affect the achievement of goals, especially within an intercultural setting.

1. *Particpants' roles and relationships to each other:*
   a. Are roles and relationships appointed, elected, inherited, earned, or assumed?
   b. Is the situation business related, educational, social, religious, or private?
   c. Are the participants family, friends, colleagues, rivals, strangers, or enemies?
   d. Are conditions intimate, casual, formal, positive, negative, neutral, mandatory, or voluntary?
   e. Is the encounter between equals or between superior and subordinate?

2. *What are some cultural variations?*
   a. How close to one another do people sit or stand?
   b. How contact oriented are people of the other culture?
   c. How long should each session take?
   d. How concentrated or superficial should the encounter be?

e. How do crossing legs, use of hands, facial expressions, and other gestures affect responses?

f. What do environment, temperature, time of day, etc., indicate?

g. How do differences between participants such as education, vocation, money, or lifestyle affect the encounter?

h. How do differences in the roles and relationships of participants affect the encounter?

i. Others?

A three-step approach (contact, continuing encounter, conclusion) will facilitate more effective communication during an intercultural encounter.

1. *The Contact.* How do you meet and relate with persons of other cultures during the initial phase of interaction? You should know these things:

a. how to use the appropriate greeting.

b. how to determine the best way to make the other person feel comfortable and responsive.

c. how to decide whether the mood should be businesslike or informal.

2. *Continuing the encounter.* You should consider the following while trying to accomplish the defined purpose with people of various cultures:

a. Attitude

i. Understand yourself before attempting to understand others. Accept yourself and others as important.

ii. Be aware that different people view their surroundings differently. Listen to and try to understand each point of view. Be tolerant; at the same time be true to yourself and your ways.

iii. Be genuinely concerned about the feelings and welfare of others.

iv. Help other people capitalize on their strengths; help them correct weaknesses that can be overcome with reasonable effort.

v. Have confidence in each person's ability to consider and choose what is best in a given situation.

  vi. Cooperatively list possible solutions (there are few perfect solutions to most of life's problems, especially between cultures).

  vii. Keep confidences, gain trust.

  viii. Always be willing to learn.

 b. Interaction

  i. Greater empathy than in many single-culture settings should be manifested. Avoid condescending attitudes, or words and gestures that might offend.

  ii. Remember that effective intercultural encounters may take more or less time (or more or fewer sessions) than anticipated and should proceed at a relaxed pace.

  iii. Simple instructions are essential. Use tact in explaining or clarifying. Help the other individual maintain self-respect.

  iv. Use the other person's manner of expression whenever necessary or possible.

  v. In general, intercultural counseling is more directive (advice giving) than nondirective (aiding self discovery or a solution).

  vi. Stay relaxed; don't let tenseness hamper the encounter. Humor varies between cultures. Learn what to use or avoid.

  vii. Try to teach the participant how to take increasingly greater responsibilities for decisions and actions.

  viii. Suspend judgment until all necessary details are available, if possible.

  ix. Do not misinterpret silence, a bowed head, or lowered eyes for hostility or shame. For many people, silence and time for reponse are valued in the communicating process as a compliment to the other person, showing that the ideas are worthy of careful consideration.

  x. Allow for periodic summaries and adequate feedback. Do all you can to show you are both "on the same wavelength."

3. *Conclusion.* To successfully complete an encounter:
   a. Summarize joint decisions.
   b. Avoid introducing potentially confusing new ideas at the last minute.
   c. Cut off at the right psychological time.
   d. Check to be sure that everybody understands, agrees with, and is committed to plans for action.

> *Sincerity: knowing how to express it is as important as having it.*
> *The same things can be expressed very differently by different people. Find out how, but do not forget why.*
>
> (Source Unknown)

Chapter 10

Communication Quick-Check

As you interact interculturally, you will need to recognize not only whether communication is acceptable or not, but also where it succeeds or breaks down and why. This quick-check can help you to understand the mechanics of your communication.

Five Vital Questions

1. What *message* do you want to communicate?
2. How *important* or *relevant* is the meassage to you and others?
3. What *conditions, customs, concerns, attitudes,* or *values* hinder or help communicate the message?
4. What specific *interpersonal* or *media* communication methods *succeed,* and *why?*
5. How do you determine message *effectiveness* and the *need* for further communication?

How to Map a Communication

The following communication elements can help you determine what is clear or ambiguous in given encounters:

[ ] *Who or What?*
(The sender, communicator, transmitter. Can be a situation or idea, a symbol or code, an oral, visual or aural message, or a person.)

[ ] *Says What?*
(The message, information, directive, idea, or code to be decoded. Watch here for mis-talk.)

[ ] *To Whom?*
(The receiver, listener, reader. Can be a nation, group, or individual, known or unknown to the sender.)

[ ] *How?*

(The medium, channel of communication. Can be a person or a form of media—radio, television, press, etc.)

[ ] Verbal   [ ] Thought

[ ] Nonverbal   [ ] Feelings

[ ] *Why?*

[ ] Tell   [ ] Convince

[ ] Inform   [ ] Sell

[ ] Teach   [ ] Entertain

[ ] Train

[ ] *Where?*

[ ] Individual reading, listening or viewing

[ ] Conversation

[ ] Classroom   [ ] Public

[ ] Meeting   [ ] Private

[ ] *When?*

[ ] Timing   [ ] Place

[ ] *Effect?*

[ ] Acceptance   [ ] Action   [ ] Learning

[ ] Interest   [ ] Feedback   [ ] Modification

[ ] Rejection   [ ] Reply   [ ] Perception

[ ] Attention   [ ] Interpretation

How to Map Mis-talk

If you or the other person in an intercultural situation did not seem to give or get a message, what was out of kilter with the communicative filter, lens, mirror, or prism that either of you were using to achieve understanding? It could be any of these:

[ ] *Mis-Talk.* You or the other person may have been talking when you should have been listening.

[ ] You did not allow for reasonable feedback.

[ ] There was too much noise or static. Other messages, whatever the source, were getting in your way.

[ ] One of you said something in error, or gave a wrong impression, and this affected feelings or behavior.

[ ] What one of you said or inferred did not have the same importance to you that it did to the other.

[ ] "Paralanguage" (body/time/space/circumstance) "said" more than you meant it to.

[ ] One or both of you lacked some ability or background in analyzing or synthesizing the other's cultural perspectives or communicative method.

[ ] *Mix-Talk*. Both of you may have been talking, thinking, doing, or going in different directions—usually because of some bias, preconceived response, or nonacceptance of the other person or the message.

How to Map Solutions

What if communication is failing? Carefully map out a solution using the following suggestions:

1. Re-listen.

2. If time is urgent, reschedule. Plan for a specific talk-through at an agreeable time and place.

3. Try the Problem-Solving Technique. Determine the following:

[ ] What is?   [ ] Who will do it?
[ ] What should be?   [ ] By when?
[ ] Why isn't it?   [ ] How to evaluate?
[ ] Where to start?   [ ] How to use
                                    effectively?

4. Use the motivating idea that the greatest enemy of your communication is its own illusion. Sort out the "real" from the "unreal." This quick-check should remind you that your communication can be enhanced by first understanding how it works, and then determining how you can best use it.

Chapter 11

How to Create and Creatively Use People-to-People Maps

> *If we reject the food, fear the religion, ignore the customs, avoid the people, we'd better stay home. We are then like a people thrown into water: wet on the surface but never part of the water.*
>
> (Source Unknown)

Maps have coordinates to help us reach destinations via the desired routes. People, too, follow routes: cultural patterns. We all have centers: values, interests, and perceptions, as well as typical expressions. We use signs and markers and colors. There are mountains and valleys in our lives, and there are rivers of change and issues that are symbolic of our apprehensions and predispositions. Some maps which we call "culture," indicate borders we protect and areas of open growth. Some maps are quite simple and lucid. Others are vague and constraining to ourselves if not to others. We are always learning—identifying new ways to get improved interactions and reactions to life. Maps are not reality: they represent places. They can be helpful, however, if used properly. We not only create people-maps, but we use them constantly, often as stereotypes, to begin associations, or to improve relationships, sometimes because we have no other way to understand.

How do we identify or "map" common yet complex challenges of intercultural understanding and behavior? How can we encourage empathy, communication, and shared ideas, and experiences? Where do you begin to understand the peoples of the world? One way for you to meet this challenge is to devise and use your own culture guides, or "people-to-people maps" for your particular needs for understanding and interaction.

The better you understand and are prepared to deal with your own and other peoples' expectations, values, and desires, the more effectively you can realistically cope with interaction challenges. If some maps do not work, new ones can be devised.

Behavior patterns for peoples emerge and comprise what we call "culture." Culture is to peoples what personality is to individuals. These patterns can be learned, appreciated, manipulated, tested, and they can often be trusted. The process of preparing people-to-people maps defines culture. Which culture(s) will you research and portray? Be specific, listing each facet or coordinate for the people groups: name, place, time, status, and how people think, feel, and behave.

How extensive will your coverage be? Collect information. Begin with yourself—your own thoughts, feelings, and experiences. Next seek appropriate and reliable experts, texts, and organizations. Make an accurate reference list for verification and future use. Sometimes we have to begin again, as in apologies, clarifications, reiteration of feelings, and emphasis.

> *Alien cultures often appear as masks but we can perceive them as garments for the spirit, appreciating their harmonies and commonalities with humanity.*
>
> (Adapted from Robert Redfield)

One major source of helpful information is natives of the culture. Be sure to obtain varied responses. Those living in the culture often have the greatest difficulty responding to questions such as we present here. They react more easily to information already gathered. Many points of view will enable more refined perspectives, especially as situations vary and conditions change.

Search and verify answers to such map-working questions as these:

1. What similarities of thought, feeling, and action are important between the information gatherer and the peoples of the culture(s) being described?

2. How do people think, feel, or act differently from you? In what circumstances?

3. How can important cultural gaps be bridged to prevent misunderstanding, offense, or embarrassment?

4. How do the described peoples expect visitors to act?

Strive for both accuracy and appropriateness. Continue by adding questions and topics to meet particular needs and situational requirements.

If your people-map seems too extensive or complex, eliminate less important information or redefine your focus. Keep the needs, interests, and priorities of map-users in mind.

Validate your information through (1) personal experience; (2) interviews with experts, (particularly a variety of people in that culture); and (3) a constant updating of basic information. Validation should be constant. Situations and people vary. Each person's interpretation of cultural behavior can differ over time and through new experiences.

> *Culture, like religion, is a mighty big word . . . Handle with care.*
>
> (Source Unknown)

How to Creatively Use People-to-People Maps

Demonstrate to other people your willingness to learn *about* them, *from* them, and *with* them. The use of people-maps confirms your desire to share this information with others, who can also learn through training workshops and seminars, travel, and various kinds of multicultural discussions.

Interpersonal relationships can be enhanced as you ask politely about situational variations such as regional, family, or individual distinctions. (Stereotypes and generalities can be useful, but they should not be specifically applied; peoples are more often alike than distinct.)

Contrasts can be used with case studies, class or group discussions, checklists, etc., to show how people are both similar and unique. Maps have different possible uses. Appreciation of several points of view can allow for profit from direct cultural contacts.

Several kinds of people-to-people maps can be studied together by comparing and contrasting the points being considered. Popular uses have been host-family programs, educational exchanges, travel tours, and the multicultural workforce.

People in multicultural situations can be led to view themselves from various perspectives (eg., as a parent, employee, or friend). We are all multicultural—influenced by a variety of roles and circumstances. This is especially true when interacting with "strangers." Your people-maps can be used for other people as well as yourself to build bridges of understanding and friendship.

Suggested People-Map Coordinates

The topics listed below can help you map peoples, using a variety of dimensions. To meet your needs, research peoples in cultures by considering the following:

1. Do they want others to live as they themselves do, or do they expect them to act according to their own cultural upbringing?

2. Is there an even "better way" for all to interact, given the situation?

3. What trends and rapidly changing lifestyles and circumstances might readers of your culture guide need to deal with broadly?

4. What are the greatest immediate and long-range needs and concerns of this culture's people? Who is realistically trying to help meet these challenges? How could other people or organizations help?

The following are representative potential coordinates for mapping peoples and their interactions:

1. *Attitudes and Values:*
    a. General expressions and perceptions (by sex, age, position).
    b. Community participation, behavior, civic pride.
    c. Cooperation vs. competition; dependence, independence, and interdependence.
    d. Crime, violence, military, police, peace initiatives.
    e. Education, classroom discipline, entry rites, status.
    f. Emotional display (empathy, affection, respect, disdain, distrust, acceptance, etc.).
    g. Fatalism vs. self-determinism, spiritual vs. materialism, etc.
    h. Friendship, commitment.
    i. Government, politics, philosophy, civil rights, welfare aids, taxes.
    j. Human nature, rationality.
    k. Humor, leisure, entertainment.
    l. Individuality in society, group expectations.
    m. Issues of human rights and other controversial concerns.
    n. Longevity, retirement, death.
    o. Majority groups, races and minorities (unique challenges, conditions).
    p. Moral codes, virtue vs. vice (promiscuity, bribery, honesty, responsibility for actions).
    q. Perceptions of nature and its powers.
    r. Politics, relations with other nations and peoples (including any generally held national attitudes toward specific nationalities).
    s. Possessions, animals, pets.
    t. Privacy, politeness.
    u. Promises, agreements; retribution.
    v. Roles (assigned or traditional).
    w. Technology, progress, change.
    x. Time orientation (past, present, future, punctuality, obligations, coordination).
    y. Treatment of elderly, handicapped, unfortunate.
    z. Wealth, material possessions, social position, class structure.
    aa. Work, obligations, success/failure, business codes, authority.

2. *Dating and Marriage*
    a.   Age standards, influence of parents and peers.
    b.   Chaperones, group sponsorship.
    c.   Common dating and courtship activities (traditions, expected behavior).
    d.   Dating individually, in groups.
    e.   Desirability of children, number, and preferences.
    f.   Display of affection.
    g.   Divorce, separation, loneliness.
    h.   Engagement customs.
    i.   Influence of family in and after marriage.
    j.   Marriage prerequisites (dowries, traditional rites, rituals).
    k.   Sexual mores.

3. *Diet*
    a.   Average diet, meal size.
    b.   Social and other occasions, places and times, scheduling.
    c.   Special foods reserved for guests or ritual occasions.
    d.   Unique problems and challenges.

4. *Economy*
    a.   Conditions and trends (inflation, interest rates, currency exchange, banking).
    b.   Methods of trade and exchange.
    c.   Relevant GNP (Gross National Product) and other contrastive statistics.

5. *Education*
    a.   Age, sex, status, literacy.
    b.   Availability, levels.
    c.   Public, private.
    d.   Systems, resources.

6. *The Family (Nuclear and Extended)*
    a.   Authority, obedience, place and expectations of children.
    b.   Daily schedules, obligations.
    c.   Entrance rites and rituals.

7. *Gestures (To Use or Avoid)*
    a.   Arms, hands, fingers (still, in motion).
    b.   Face (eye contact, motion, smiling or frowning).
    c.   Handling, passing, receiving.

    d. Legs and feet (still, motion).
    e. Posture (formal, informal).
    f. Touching, embracing.

8. *Greetings, Leave-Taking, and Farewell*
    a. Names, and titles (status).
    b. New people, everyday acquaintances, close friends.
    c. Men, women, children, aged.
    d. Leaders, followers, employees, groups.
    e. Compliments (given, received; formality, sincerity).
    f. Space (standing, sitting, distance between people).
    g. Time (promptness, duration).
    h. Turn taking (who speaks to whom, when, how long?).

9. *Health*
    a. Health care availability and technology.
    b. Life expectancy, infant mortality, disease.
    c. Sanitation, concerns.

10. *History and Government*
    a. Important events and facts considered most important, traditional, exclusive.
    b. Heroes and leaders (historic, contemporary, favored, disfavored).
    c. Political and civil rights, responsibilities and liberties (voting, holding office, "freedom").
    d. Systems (national, regional, local; socio-economical, political).

11. *Special Holidays, Holy Days, and Social Rituals*
    a. Ceremonies: private, public.
    b. Dates and observances.
    c. Traditions, showing respect.

12. *Land and Climate*
    a. Geographical effects on history, living conditions, and lifestyles.
    b. Seasons (temperatures, weather conditions).
    c. Size, attractions.

13. *Languages (Official, Informal, Vernacular, What to Avoid, Change, Plural Uses)*
    a. Favorite, familiar, pleasing phrases.
    b. Nonverbal (see also *gestures*).

c. Paranormal (the "unspoken," "vibes," intuition, etc.).
d. Paraverbal (rate, pitch, tone; spacing size, etc.).
e. Verbal (spoken, written, and non-fluencies).

14. *Meetings and Interviews*
    a. Beginnings and endings (local format, duration).
    b. Formality, audience.
    c. Seating arrangements, eye contact, posture, alertness.

15. *Personal Appearance (appropriateness)*
    a. Clothing (formal, informal).
    b. Grooming.
    c. Use and misuse of native dress.

16. *Population (Trends, Impact on Economics, etc.)*
    a. Predominant, minority.
    b. Rural, suburban, urban.
    c. Ratios of age, sex, etc.

17. *Public Addresses and Conversation*
    a. Mannerisms that are or are not appropriate.
    b. Subjects and illustrations to discuss or avoid; timing.
    c. Use of interpreters and translators—recognition, appreciation.

18. *Recreation, Leisure, Sports, and Arts*
    a. Distinctive arts and sciences visitors should be familiar with.
    b. Family, cultural, and social recreation, vacations, sports.
    c. Individual recreation, games.
    d. Well-known artists, athletes.

19. *Religion and Philosophy Specifics*
    a. Predominant, minority.
    b. Cosmology, world views, animism, agnosticism, atheism.
    c. Devotional rites and rituals, those of passage.
    d. Clergy, expectations of members, volunteerism.
    e. Myths, luck, taboos.

20. *Social and Economic Levels*
    a. Classes, average income.
    b. Housing and possessions.
    c. Poverty and wealth, care of the less fortunate.
    d. Symbols of status.

21. *Transportation and Communication*
    a. Individual, group travel (facilities, costs, availability; egs., train/plane/boat).
    b. Mass-communication media (television, radio, newspapers, magazines, telephones).
    c. Networks.
    d. Postal systems.
    e. Road systems (public, private access).

22. *Visiting (Formal and Informal)*
    a. Business and other focused discussions (time, place, setting).
    b. Calling cards or other follow-up aids, such as thank you notes.
    c. Compliments on possessions, family, local or national circumstances.
    d. Conversation (topics, appropriate time during visit).
    e. Gifts (giving, receiving; tokens of respect).
    f. Parties and other social events (unique behavior expectations).

23. *Words and Phrases*
    a. Formalities and diplomacy.
    b. Survival phrases.
    c. Traditional key words and phrases.
    d. Idioms, cliches, slang.

24. *Work and Work Schedules*
    a. Ability, opportunity for advancement.
    b. Environment, climate, conditions.
    c. Machinery, tools available, technology.
    d. Main and unique occupations, industries, products.
    e. Recompense; self or other employment.
    f. Training and development programs.
    g. Work schedules (hours, days), vacations.

25. *Miscellaneous*
    a. Accommodations (public, private, reservations, costs).
    b. Eating (table manners, utensils, grace, meal schedules).
    c. Photographing (laws, courtesies).
    d. Shopping (store sizes and locations, prices, business hours and availability, exchange rates).

  e. Tipping (when, who, how much).
  f. Traveling (tourist sites, group programs, maps).
26. *Other People-Map Coordinates You Feel Are Important*

> *Shall we ever cease our explorations*
> *So that the end thereof will be*
> *To arrive where once we started—*
> *And know the place and the people*
> *For the first time?*
>
> (Adapted from T.S. Eliot)

Chapter 12

Resources for Mapping
People and Their Interactions

Getting Specific Help for Intercultural Interactions

For starters, visit the closest major library and ask a reference librarian for assistance in locating general worldwide or regional sources. *Encyclopedia Britannica* offers a two-to-three page demographic, historic, geographic and social country profile, which provides the most important data of a country. The most current demographic data is provided in the *Britannica Book of the Year/Annual World Data*.

Europe Publications Limited publishes a series of regional studies (Africa South of the Sahara, Europe, The Far East and Australia, and Central and South America). Each volume provides a succinct overview of each country in the area covered, and includes a helpful directory and bibliographic references.

For more than 20 years, the American University in Washington, D.C., has published *Country Profiles*—previously called *Area Handbooks* . These are now available from the Federal Research Division, Library of Congress, Washington, D.C. Each volume covers one country or geographic region. Even though some of the volumes are dated, they contain valuable historical and cultural information.

For a more comprehensive source, see Kohls, L. Robert and V. Lynn Tyler. *A Select Guide to Area Studies Resources*. Provo, Utah: Brigham Young University, David M. Kennedy Center for International Studies, 1988.

Other major reference texts available in large city or university libraries include *Stateman's Yearbook, Cities of the World,* or *Travel Book: Guide to the Travel Guides*. The comprehensive Banana

Republic Travel Bookstore Catalog is available by calling (800) 772-9977.

Additional bibliographic sources which are updated annually include the *World Bibliographic Series, World Bank Economic Reports, The World Factbook, Background Notes on the Countries of the World, The International Yearbook,* and *Stateman's Who's Who.*

Directories list embassies, foreign and cultural-support services, and international organizations that are often willing to exchange or share current, pertinent information. *The Encyclopedia of Associations, Yearbooks of International Organizations,* and *Books in Print* are also helpful resources that a librarian can help you use.

The most specific source for certain people studies is probably the *Human Relations Area Files.* The *Outline of World Cultures* is the index for the microfiche material and covers almost every country of the world—though the data may be rather dated. The microfiche series is divided by ethnic group.

Contact embassies, domestic and foreign travel agencies, tourist services, and regional and international organizations. They are often willing to provide current country-specific information, or to help you find experts who can.

Many time-saving computer-aided research systems are now available. Ask about the Institute for Scientific Information, BRS, CompuServe, DIALOG, Nexis, SDC, The Source, or whatever your library has. The cost is often unexpectedly low for what is available. A thesaurus of terms can narrow the topic and facilitate a search.

Publishers such as McDougal-Littel, McGraw-Hill, Sage, Time-Life, and Couriers all feature texts or series on different cultures of the world. Direct distributors of international and intercultural materials include the Social Studies School Service's Global Education catalog (P.O. Box 802, Culver City, CA 90230), Global Perspectives in Education Access (218 East 18th Street, New York, NY 10003; 213-475-0850), and Intercultural Press, Inc. (P.O. Box 768, Yarmouth, ME 04096; 207-846-5168).

Work with your local university anthropologists, area or language professors, cross-cultural psychologists, and multicultural education specialists for your specific information needs.

The International Society for Intercultural Education, Training, and Research (1505 22nd Street, N.W., Washington, D.C. 20037;

202-296-4710) is a professional association devoted to the cause of international understanding and appropriate intercultural interaction.

You are your best resource. Build on your own experience while using the latest and best resource aids: people, ideas, material, and experience.

Your Suggestions and Recommendations

Others can benefit from your experience and insights. Please let us know how you use your guides, and how you modify and refine them. We welcome your candor, criticism, and commentary. Please write if we can share research. Contact V. Lynn Tyler, Brigham Young University, David M. Kennedy Center for International Studies, 273 HRCB, Provo, UT 84602, 801–378–2652.

We are continually exploring and mapping people-to-people frontiers. The David M. Kennedy Center for International Studies publishes *Culturgrams* and *Infograms*. *Culturgrams* are four-page briefings on ninety-six countries or areas. *Infograms* are briefings on topics of general international and intercultural interest. For a free catalogue and a sample *Culturgram,* contact Brigham Young University, David M. Kennedy Center for International Studies, Publication Services, 280 HRCB, Provo, Utah 84602, 801–378–6528.

To be successful as people ambassadors to people, we cannot stop at "knowing about others." We recognize similarities that are significant, and we bridge differences that make a difference in customs, goals, and patterns and styles of thought and emotion.

Interaction is obviously more than a simple two-way street between two cultures. Rather, it is a busy intersection at which at least five thoroughfares meet: the two language backgrounds with all their eccentricities, the worldviews of the two communities being represented, and the intended situation for which the interaction is in process.

(Adapted from Peter Farb, in memorium)